"If you want valuable guidance on how to succeed in business and, more importantly, how to succeed in life, then Life with Flavor *is a must read. Meet Jim Herr and learn. And whatever you do, do NOT skip Mim's Notes in the Epilogue!"*

President George F

"It's more than a blueprint for a delicious chip and successful business. Jim's words offer an inspiring recipe for a fulfilling life of faith, family and community."

Governor Tom Ridge, Former Governor of Pennsylvania
First Secretary, U.S. Department of Homeland Security

∽∾

"One of the great blessings of ministry is meeting people that exemplify living life to its fullest. Jim Herr is such a man. So it is fitting that he entitled his new book Life with Flavor. *For those who have family businesses or have a desire to start a business, or for those who just want to be inspired by a story of turning hardships into victories or heartaches into blessings, this book is for you. Jim Herr and his entire family have a story that will touch hearts as accounts are given to what the Lord will do in lives that are committed to Him. Many dream of spicing up their lives. I encourage readers to consider how Jim Herr found favor with God and how his faithfulness to God's Word flavored his life."*

Franklin Graham, President and CEO
Billy Graham Evangelistic Association and Samaritan's Purse

"My wife and I sought the advice and counsel of Jim and Mim Herr around their breakfast table before I first ran for public office.

Their life story is both inspiring and instructional on not only how to build a successful business but how to live a productive life. Young entrepreneurs and small businesses would do well to emulate their example of ethical stewardship and good judgment.

This is a short book full of lessons learned from a life well-lived."

Congressman Joseph R. Pitts
16th Congressional District, Pennsylvania

∽o∾

"The world is a beautiful place when nice guys finish first. James Stauffer Herr is one of the nicest people in the world. Jim's story personifies the American dream that hard work, perseverance and an entrepreneurial spirit are the ingredients for success.

I have known Jim for close to 40 years. Our company became a customer of Herr's shortly after opening our first store on April 16th, 1964. Over this period Herr's has often been rated by our store managers as providing the best service of all Direct Store Delivery vendors and is consistently rated in the top 10%. While the business success of Herr's is much to be admired, the relationship of their family to the business and to each other is equally remarkable. Most family businesses fall on hard times in the 2nd or 3rd generation; Herr's is built to last because of the values that Jim and Mim have instilled in their family. If you like stories of people with a passion for the Lord, a desire to help others and a happy ending, read Life with Flavor!"

Dick Wood, Chairman, Wawa

"As I read the book Life with Flavor, *this thought keeps recurring: Jim and his Lady, Mim, reflect the life of their Lord, who was filled "with grace and truth." Sometimes, people who major on graciousness fudge on the truth, and people who major on truth can be brittle and even unkind.*

In this compelling volume you read the story of a man who, without trimming his stated convictions, built a world class business. I have traveled around the world with Jim and Mim, and they live out their "grace and truth" commitment 24/7. May God give this book wide broadcast."

John Haggai, Founder and Chairman, Haggai Institute

∞o∞

"What a wonderful book! No one better demonstrates all that has made our country great than Jim Herr. He created a successful business by following the principles of honesty, humility, integrity and old fashioned hard work … all guided by a strong faith.

There are no better examples for all of us to be successful in business and in life than those in this book. Jim Herr's wisdom and experience is a great gift to anyone who reads Life with Flavor.*"*

Dan Danner, President
National Federation of Independent Business

∞o∞

"Over the years the Phillies have enjoyed teaming up with another Philly favorite, Herr's Snack Foods. Jim's book contains the details of hits, homeruns and a few errors in the company he founded."

Bill Giles, Chairman, Philadelphia Phillies

"I would like to offer the appreciation of the entire snack food industry to Mr. James S. Herr for his leadership and devotion to the Snack Food Association and the industry he helped build. He has always believed that the association's principle duty is to ensure that our industry is well represented in the corridors of government so that the entrepreneurial spirit that made our industry strong is not forgotten.

I want to congratulate Jim Herr on this autobiography of his great life and work. In short, Jim is a highly respected businessman who created his successful company through honest hard work, devotion to family, dedication to his country and a strong belief in God. The snack industry will always be grateful to Jim Herr for sharing his wisdom and great talents in building our association and industry."

James McCarthy, President and CEO
Snack Food Association

Life with Flavor

A Personal History of Herr's

James S. Herr, Founder

with Bruce E. Mowday

and June Herr Gunden

Fort Lee, New Jersey

Published by Barricade Books, Fort Lee, New Jersey

PRINTED IN THE UNITED STATES OF AMERICA
By DavCo Advertising, Inc., Kinzers, Pennsylvania

Cover Design by Herr Foods Design Team
Text Design by Anita W. Taylor
Editorial Services by Peachtree Editorial Service, Peachtree City, Georgia
Pictures from Herr's 65th Anniversary DVD Courtesy of AVIO Productions

Hardback: ISBN 13 9781569804698
             ISBN 10 1569804699

Paperback: ISBN 13 9781569805145
             ISBN 10 1569805148

Library of Congress Cataloging-in-Publication Data
Herr, James Stauffer, 1924-2012
  Life with Flavor! : A Personal History of Herr's / by James S. Herr with Bruce E. Mowday and June Herr Gunden.
    p. cm.
  Includes bibliographical references.
  ISBN 978-1-56980-469-8
  1. Herr, James Stauffer, 1924- 2012. Herr family. 3. Herr Foods (Firm)–History. 4. Businesspeople–United States–Biography. 5. Food industry and trade–United States. I. Mowday, Bruce. II. Gunden, June. III. Title.
  HD9000.9.U5H397 2012
  338.7'6646--dc23
            2012012371

First printing

Printed on acid free paper.

Dedicated to the memory of James S. Herr,

the founder and inspiration of Herr Foods Inc.,

who died April 5, 2012,

after the manuscript was completed.

This posthumous autobiography honors the career

and life of a remarkable man.

TABLE OF CONTENTS

ACKNOWLEDGMENTS

Just as our business was built by the efforts of many, this book came about through many people. I am actually not the writer, but I am the author of the content, in that it records my thoughts and my life's message.

The research has come from Bruce E. Mowday, who interviewed many of our family members, employees, and associates, and he compiled a draft of the material. It was then re-shaped and put into my words by my daughter June and her husband, Doug, who have a business that provides editorial services. From there, other members of our family fine-tuned it, so it is truly a joint effort.

I thank all who gave of their memories and their efforts to make this book possible.

James S. Herr

INTRODUCTION

Many people like the idea of building something from nothing. In business, the one who builds an enterprise from scratch is called an entrepreneur, and that's how I'm often labeled.

I didn't necessarily set out to become an entrepreneur—I didn't even know that was an option—but perhaps the idea appeals to you. Perhaps you would like to start a business or expand an enterprise and you wonder, "How could I do that? Could you give me any tips?"

Whatever I have learned along the way I will be happy to share with you. As I tell my story, I'll summarize some key principles that you may find helpful. I would like to encourage you to accomplish all that you personally were created to do, because that's when you truly live life with zest and purpose—with *flavor*.

I believe the Great Creator is the model entrepreneur. Starting from nothing, He made the whole world! Afterwards, the Bible says, He made human beings "in His own image." He made us to be creative and to work hard at something, just like He did. That's why I think we instinctively admire these values.

The book of Proverbs has greatly influenced my thinking as a business person. Throughout my story I will share some of the practical words of advice in it, as they relate to decisions or situations I've faced (they are taken from *Living Psalms and Proverbs*, by Dr. Kenneth Taylor).

I hope that something I say will spark that inborn gift God created within you, so that you can be encouraged in your life's work and live life with flavor!

Prologue

HERR FOODS TODAY

First I'll tell you a little bit about Herr's today.

The main products we sell are potato chips, pretzels, popcorn, cheese curls, tortilla chips, pork rinds, crackers, and nuts. We manufacture about 85 percent of these products. Our stated mission is to increase sales profitably by safely providing the best products and service available.

If you live in our area of the country (the mid-Atlantic, Greater Philadelphia region) you may be familiar with our turquoise, red, and white route sales trucks. They are one of our best assets because of the relationships and the service they represent. Local store managers want to buy products from someone who knows and cares about their business and personally delivers fresh products. The Herr's salesperson keeps the store's shelves stocked and introduces the manager to our new products, which contributes to the store's success. Today we have more than 500 routes operating from 20 warehouses and two plants, and I think the best way to learn about what Herr's is all about is to operate one of those routes. That is the "ground floor" of our operation.

Of course, Herr's gets calls all the time from other areas of the country, and we want to grow, so we have developed other methods of sales. One is national sales, where our sales people work with retailers who have chain stores nationwide. This is a growing part of our business, and we hope that in the future we will become much more well-known across our country. Our export business is also growing rapidly, so maybe you'll see our product when you travel overseas.

Right now we have about 1,500 employees. We work hard to maintain healthy relationships and two-way communication, and I'm pleased that there are no unions involved. To me that would be an indication that our management team is not doing a good job of fostering our culture of being "one family" of people, striving together to build a better company. Our goal is to continue that culture, which I believe explains why we have so many long-term employees.

In 2013, Herr Foods Inc., with annual sales of over $250 million, ranked in the top five of independently-owned salty snack food companies in the country.

But Herr's today is very different from anything I anticipated as a young man. Let me tell you a little about my early life.

Jim as a teenager on his dad's farm

Chapter 1

I KNEW WHAT I *DIDN'T* WANT TO DO

I was born on August 6, 1924, and raised in the village of Willow Street, Pennsylvania, a farming community south of Lancaster. I was the second child born to Ira L. and Mary Stauffer Herr. (My middle name is Stauffer, after Mom's maiden name.) There were five children in my family: Christian, me, Mary, Ira, and Anna Mae.

My father purchased our 86-acre farm in 1925 for $5,000. During my early childhood our nation was going through the Great Depression. My dad would often remind us, "Don't spread the butter too thick." You could make the butter last by not using a lot at one time. It was a time to be frugal, very frugal. I'm not saying we suffered when we were spreading the butter thin. Since we were farmers, we had enough to eat and we did not experience some of the ravaging effects of the Depression that others in our country suffered. But we were very careful about how we earned and spent money.

My perception was that we were poor compared to some of my buddies' families. Their dads' farms seemed to have plenty of tractors and cars. Whenever my family got a car, it would already be five years old or so. We didn't have a tractor until I was a teenager and then we got a used Fordson row crop tractor. I used to plow with mules, not horses, before we got the Fordson.

My father was a conservative man. He believed that all of his children should work on the farm until we were 21 years old and then we could decide what career we wanted to pursue. Before that time, if we made money in some other way, such as doing a task for a neighbor, we were expected to give the money to our parents to be used for family expenses.

"Pop" also believed the boys should be given a car for working on the farm. (The girls were given comparable money toward household items.) One of the most important times for a boy was when he turned 16 and was able to drive a car. Having driven the farm vehicles, I knew how to drive before I was 16. But I didn't get my first car—a used 1940 Olds Cruiser—until I was 19 years old.

My childhood was nurtured by working with my family on the farm, spending time with our large extended family, and attending regular worship services at Willow Street Mennonite Church. Our heritage in the Mennonite church was a huge factor in how our family lived our lives. In fact, I'll share with you a little bit more about Mennonites, to help you understand why we thought the way we did.

Mennonites are Protestants who are traditionally pacifists and choose options other than the military to serve our country. We are known for traits like humility, thriftiness, and concern for others (especially in areas such as disaster relief). At the time I grew up there was also a major emphasis on living a simple way of life, shunning materialism, and being separate from the values of the surrounding culture (the "world"). In our area, being separate meant that we dressed differently from others—you could easily tell who was a Mennonite and who wasn't. We were encouraged to stay separate, to be "plain" and not "worldly," and not to engage too much in the larger culture in such ways as voting in elections.

Some people link us to the Amish, but the Amish are a completely different group. Unlike them, Mennonites do not object to modern conveniences and transportation methods. No longer do most Mennonites live on the farm and stay as separate from the larger culture as the Amish do. And the people in our family do not dress differently any more, though some Mennonite groups still do.

At the time I was growing up, my family valued hard work above formal education. Perhaps my parents were afraid that education would cause their children to stray from the simple way of life and to become more like the "world," rather than staying separated from it. My father did not think it was necessary for us to go to high school, and he felt he needed us to help on the farm; accordingly, after I began the ninth grade, he encouraged me to quit school. Though I enjoyed school, and I especially loved to play basketball there, I went along with my father's wishes. I trusted that he knew what was best for me, and it was gratifying to know I was needed and that I was old enough to do a man's job.

Each child on the Herr farm was responsible for a specific area of work, though of course we all had to help wherever we were needed. My special job was to take care of the poultry operation, a task I

*Tobacco Shed, early site of
Herr's Potato Chips*

Herr Farm, Willow Street, PA

came to dislike, because there was no one to talk to all day long but chickens! We had about 2,000 laying hens at the time, and I had to clean the eggs. My brothers took care of our herd of cows, which numbered eleven or twelve.

We also grew a number of crops on the farm, such as corn, soybeans, wheat, and grass for the hay. We grew tobacco at one time, but eventually we stopped, mostly as a matter of conscience. My parents didn't approve of smoking, so even though growing tobacco was lucrative, they decided we shouldn't be growing it. We changed to tomatoes instead, and we sold our crop to Campbell's for making soup.

A typical day for me began about 5:00 A.M. I would help do the milking and then eat breakfast, before starting the rest of the daily farm chores. This was pretty much the norm for all of us and we didn't think it was unusual to work long days, especially when the crops or herds demanded it.

Some of the good times I remember centered on going to farm shows, local fairs, and family gatherings. I especially enjoyed playing ball with cousins and neighbors. As a teenager I decided I wanted to play the guitar and found a good local teacher, Howard Simmons. He had an "orchestra" of stringed instruments that would perform here and there and I loved playing in it. I still enjoy a good bluegrass band playing tunes such as "The Orange Blossom Special," "The Wabash Cannonball," and "The Wreck of the Old 97."

Our church was also a social outlet for us young people. Periodically there would be special meetings, when evangelistic speakers would come in from other areas, and they would preach a series of sermons encouraging people to come to faith in Christ. These "revivals" were usually held once a year, every night for about two weeks. They were always a social highlight for me, because for all those evenings in a row I got to be with my buddies and my cousins.

During those meetings, each evening an "invitation" would be given to anyone who wanted to dedicate their life to follow Christ and His teaching. When I was twelve I had a feeling that I should respond. I waited until the last night of the meetings and the last part of the invitation (I guess I was hesitant to take this big step), and then I stood up to be acknowledged as a Christian. It was a decision that would shape the rest of my life, as you will see throughout my story.

One of the things the church taught us was to learn to appreciate the Bible, as God's guidebook for living. When I was 15, I decided I would try to read through the book of Psalms and one verse in particular got my attention. Here is what Psalm 37:4 says:

Delight yourself in the Lord
And He will give you the desires of your heart.

I thought, "Boy, now that's a great promise! When the Maker of the Universe promises to give me the desires of my heart, I'm going to take Him up on it!"

I knew that I had a lot of desires in my heart (like getting away from the isolation of cleaning eggs and feeding chickens), and I took the Lord at His word and believed that He would give those to me, if I

Mim, age 11

would "delight myself" in Him. What exactly did that mean? I wasn't sure, but I made an agreement with Him, that I would learn to delight myself in Him. I had faith that He would give me my heart's desires.

I didn't know it at the time, but one of the eventual "desires of my heart" lived on a nearby farm. There a young girl was growing up who would be my life's partner.

"Mim" (Miriam Esther Hershey), who is now my wife of 64 years, was born on November 29, 1926, to Isaac Hershey, Jr., and Esther Burkhart Hershey in Paradise, Pennsylvania. Just like me, she was raised on a farm, in a Mennonite family in Lancaster County, as the second oldest in her family. She was even named for her mother, just like me.

Her family was all girls for many years. Her parents had three daughters and then twins—also daughters. In a farm family you are looking for boys to help with the work, but those five girls learned how to work hard. They milked cows, fed chickens, harvested potatoes, hoed corn, and picked the worms off of tobacco leaves. Eventually Mim's parents had twin sons and then a third son, making a total of eight children.

Mim's family's farm in Paradise, Pennsylvania, had 70 or 80 acres, big enough to make a living for their large family. The property didn't have a stream, so each day at noon the children helped bring in all the cows so they could drink water. Both of us learned early in our lives that as a farm family you had to "pull together" and do what needed to be done, regardless of whether you felt like doing it.

We also learned that you get a sense of satisfaction when you can see tangible results from your hard work. Many of the farms in Lancaster County are known even today for their neatness, because people take pride in caring for their property. Maybe we found it tedious to weed the corn, or mow the hay, or paint the fence, but at the end of the day we saw the results of our efforts. We knew we had accomplished something.

There wasn't a lot of recreation in Mim's family life, but sometimes in the evening their Dad would play a little softball with them; or in the winter, if they had time, they would go sledding. Her father was a strict disciplinarian; he regularly drilled the children on their multiplication tables and memory work, often at the dinner table. They were expected to do their best in school. He was also fond of music and he made sure each of his eight children learned to play the piano. Some evenings the family would gather around the piano and sing as he played hymns. They attended the Paradise Mennonite Church every week; like my family, her family was very committed to their faith.

Mim became a Christian when she was 15 and she remembers that the catalyst was a bicycle accident. She was riding her bicycle (actually she shared it with her sister) along Route 30 (busy even at that time) after a snow storm. She couldn't see where the cement stopped and the gravel shoulder started, and when the wheels hit the gravel, they slipped out from under her. She was thrown from the bike into a lane of traffic, her school books flying all over the place. Fortunately the traffic on the road could swerve around her, but after that close call she thought she should get more serious about her relationship with God. Like me, she made a public commitment to Christ in her church and her Christian faith was nurtured there.

It's ironic that Mim sold potato chips before I did—and those of a future competitor! At that time farmers would travel to a "farmer's market" in a larger city to sell their produce, supplemented by other items they made or bought for re-sale. In her early teens Mim often spent Saturdays in Philadelphia, leaving before dawn to get there in time to work at a stand that sold things like starter plants for people's gardens, fresh vegetables, pretzels, and potato chips. The chips, which came from Utz, in Hanover, Pennsylvania, were sold at the farmer's market by the ounce. Mim scooped the chips from a large container and placed them in waxed bags for the customers. I'm sure she never dreamed that one day she'd be scooping Herr's potato chips into bags!

At the age of 15, while a sophomore and an excellent student, Mim decided to stop attending high school. The reason may seem odd to you, but I think it's interesting how our life choices affect the future in ways we can't anticipate. At that time it was her perception that when she became a Christian (as I've described above) she would need to start dressing like a Mennonite. She had observed that those in her school who dressed this way were not popular, and she didn't want to face her peers, now that she was going to start dressing "plain." So she just told them she wouldn't be back.

She went home and told her father that she wanted to quit school. Apparently he didn't object and took her to the local magistrate's office to sign the papers for her to quit school early. The official said,

"OK, I assume it's because you need her on the farm."

"No," her father replied honestly. "I don't need her on the farm. She just wants to quit."

"Well, you could just sign the paper anyway, because we need a reason on record."

But her father insisted that he wouldn't sign any such paper because it wasn't true—he didn't need her on the farm.

Mim was appalled. Sitting on the edge of the imposing arm chair nearby, she begged him, "Dad, you *have* to sign those papers. I *can't* go back. I told all the girls I wouldn't be back." But her father was not going to lie.

The magistrate must have seen how desperate she was, so he suggested, "Is there something else that we could give for a reason, like do you want to go to a different school or something? What are you good at?"

Mim had always had an idea that she wanted to be a secretary. She told the magistrate that she was good at numbers (remember all those multiplication drills at the Hershey dinner table) and she thought she would like to learn to type.

The magistrate suggested that she could go to a business school and she jumped at the chance. At least no one there would know her or care that she was dressing "plain." Plus she really was an excellent student and the idea of more schooling appealed to her.

So it was that she set out to enroll in Lancaster Business College. She tells it this way: "I remember it was a Friday night that my dad called the school. Dad was told that the school usually didn't accept students without a high school diploma, but he assured them that I was a very good student. Well, they said, if I came to the school the next Monday, someone would be available to talk to me and maybe they would give it a try. Dad had other obligations that Monday, but he gave me a quarter for the round-trip bus fare to the school on North Queen Street in Lancaster.

"What an unnerving day! I used the quarter to ride the bus into the city and somehow found the school. There a bookkeeping teacher met me and said I could sit in on his class; he said it would cost 25 cents for the textbook. Embarrassed that I had already used my quarter and had no more money, I must have looked pretty unsettled. Kindly, he told me if it was inconvenient I could bring the payment in the next day.

"Sitting there in my homemade cotton dress (I can still visualize the corduroys and jackets of the other students), aware that everyone else was older and had graduated from high school, I still somehow tuned in when the teacher gave the class an oral math question. I computed the answer in my head while the other students were working it out on paper, and I waited for one of them to give the answer. No hands went up. Hmmm, maybe I was wrong. Computing it again, I felt sure it was the correct answer. Timidly I raised my hand and the teacher seemed surprised when I gave the correct answer.

" 'Miss Hershey, how did you arrive at the answer so quickly?' he asked.

" 'I used algebra.' (It was the math course I had been taking as a sophomore in high school.)

"The other students looked at me quizzically. Sure, they had taken algebra in high school, but this was several years later and this was bookkeeping. I'm sure they wondered where this little plain Mennonite girl came from who had wandered into their classroom. I never made many friends there (they were all older and much more sophisticated), but I felt like I could hold my own when it came to the school work, and the teachers must have agreed, because they let me stay, even without my high school diploma.

"After that first day of school, I couldn't remember where the bus stop was and stood on the wrong corner for what seemed like hours. Eventually I saw a lady who looked approachable and I asked her where the bus stop was. She smiled sympathetically and said 'I'll just walk you there,' probably realizing I'd never make it otherwise. My mother was nearly frantic by the time I made it home. But the mission was accomplished, and I was enrolled in a 15-month secretarial course. There I learned typing, bookkeeping, shorthand, and became qualified to work as a legal secretary."

As I look back on Mim's unusual decision to go to business school, I can't help but think the Lord was preparing her already for the future life we would lead together in our business. Typing invoices, keeping track of accounts, organizing the ledgers, filling out tax forms—who would have done all that if it hadn't been for her? She is a meticulous bookkeeper of our personal finances to this day and I know better than to question whether she has paid a bill on time. She also has her father's dogged determination to do everything by the book, not to fudge for convenience or to use the ends to justify the means. I think God honors that integrity.

I actually met Mim by dating her older sister. I had a couple of dates with Evelyn before I found out that I was a "test." She'd had a steady boyfriend before we met and they had decided to date other people before committing to an engagement. After she dated me a few times, she realized that I wasn't the one she wanted!

It could have been pretty devastating to me, except that during one of those dates, I saw Mim at a church function and realized I didn't have *my* first choice either. Mim must have thought I looked OK, too, so we were both glad it worked out that way.

Neither of us had dated many people before we met each other—I was only 19 and she was 17. Dates at that time were often double dates to church events; afterwards we'd go to friends' homes to have a snack and maybe play Rook (a card game popular in our circles at that time) or some other game. Sometimes we went to a sports event or a local fair or farm show, but not often.

During this time I was still working on my father's farm and Mim was going to business college. Later, she began working for a friend of her father, an attorney in Lancaster named Samuel Wenger.

My father had always said we could stop working on the farm when we were 21, so as soon as I celebrated my 21st birthday, I decided I would talk to him. I told my dad that poultry farming was too lonely for me —I didn't have anyone to talk with during the day. I wanted to try another profession. He was fine with my decision, but he said he didn't have any money to help me get started.

So the first thing that started me on my entrepreneurial journey was that I knew I wanted to do something that would get me off the farm so that I could interact more with people. And I had that promise from Psalm 37:4. But without any money or education, what would it be?

Continue to reverence the Lord all the time,
for surely you have a wonderful future ahead of you.
There is hope for you yet!
Proverbs 23:17, 18

Business Principles

If you are in a profession you don't enjoy, be willing to make a change. I've known people who resign themselves to a job they detest and then complain about it their whole lives.

Learn to enjoy the satisfaction that comes from working hard and seeing tangible results.

The lazy man is full of excuses. "I can't go to work!" he says.
"If I go outside I might meet a lion in the street and be killed!"

Proverbs 22:13

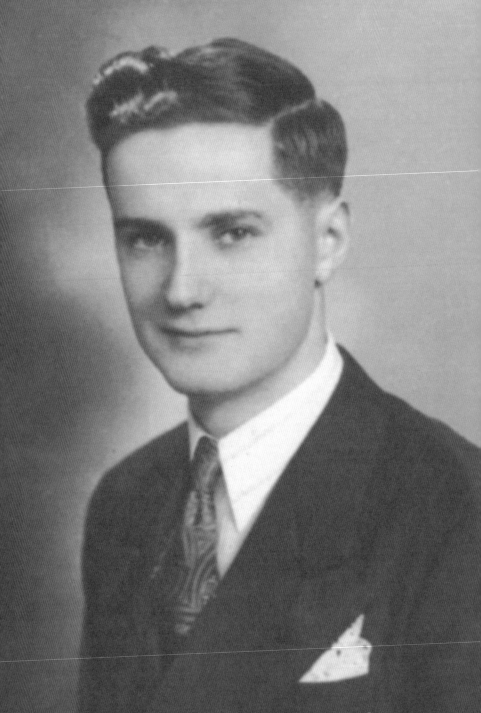

Jim, age 21

Chapter 2

AN OPPORTUNITY FOR CHANGE

Every day I would sit and clean eggs, eggs, and more eggs. And every day I would eagerly search the newspaper for leads on a different kind of job. I started looking in August (right after my birthday) and I believe it was March of the next year before I saw anything that I thought would be remotely feasible.

I saw that a potato chip business was for sale in Lancaster that cost $1,750.00. Now, I didn't have any attraction to potato chips, because snacking was not common in our home—we were too frugal for that. But it struck me that here was a business that seemed doable and affordable.

∞

The intelligent man is always open to new ideas.
In fact, he looks for them.
Proverbs 18:15

∞

Not that I had the money, or knew anything about going to a bank and getting a loan. My Dad always took care of the finances for our family and I didn't know that getting a bank loan was an option.

If I were looking to start a business today, I might make use of a resource like the Small Business Administration, which was founded by an act of Congress in 1953 to "aid, counsel, assist and protect, insofar as is possible, the interests of small business concerns." Over the years, Herr's has looked to the SBA for loans and help with growing our company. I would encourage you, if you are interested in starting a business, to go to their website, *www.SBA.gov*, for help.

But if the SBA had existed in 1946, I probably wouldn't have known about it. As I was thinking of how I could get the cash I needed, a possibility came to mind—maybe I could ask Mim's boss to loan me the money. I knew that he was a successful attorney and I thought he might be willing to give me a chance to get started.

Without further ado (and without mentioning it to Mim), I told the owners I thought I'd be interested and took them to Mr. Wenger's office to see if he would give me a loan.

Mim tells about that day in 1946, when I went to ask for the loan, like this: "I was in my side office of the law firm, where I could see

Mim, age 19

the main area of the office, and I saw a young man come into the room with a buxom peroxide blonde. To my surprise, Jim was with them! The three of them said they wanted to see Mr. Wenger. Jim waltzed right by me with the couple and entered Mr. Wenger's office. Mr. Wenger came out of his office some minutes later and told me to write out a note for $1,750 to Mr. Herr. I was thinking, 'What on earth is Jim doing with that couple and why does he need money?' Jim came by my desk and said, 'I'll call you tonight.' I was thinking, 'You bet you will.' "

When I saw Mim that night I told her of my plan to purchase Verna's Potato Chips, located on Charlotte Street in Lancaster. For my investment of $1,750, I would receive two iron kettles, each capable of holding one hundred pounds of lard, a three-potato slicer, a peeler that held ten pounds of potatoes, and a 1936 Dodge panel truck in fair condition. The deal also included a part-time employee and a rented building.

Iron kettle used in the Lancaster location and tobacco shed

Mim knew how much I wanted to get a job where I could be around people instead of sitting by myself and cleaning eggs. Still, when I first told her of my plans, she thought the idea was way off the wall. What did we know about making potato chips? All I knew was, I had to repay that loan, or I'd not only lose the business but I'd lose my girlfriend as well.

The former owners, neither of whom was "Verna," promised to stay on the job for two weeks to teach me the business. Two days after the sale was completed, however, they abruptly departed and I never saw them again.

After being in the chip business for about three months, I wasn't sure if I had made the right decision in selecting my new profession.

I found the work very greasy and tedious. However, I knew I had an obligation to Samuel Wenger, and I was bound to keep my word.

It was about this time that I asked Mim to marry me. As I look back, I think about how she accepted who I was even though my career must have seemed quite shaky. I didn't like the farm, and I wasn't sure I liked the chip business—did she ever wonder if I would be a stable provider?

Also, during our dating years I battled depression periodically. Not only was I not happy in my job on the farm, but I was quite conflicted over my military exemption (an agricultural deferment), during a time when many of my neighborhood friends were being sent to Europe to fight in World War II. I felt it was unfair that they were risking their lives and I was just going about my normal life. Though our church was traditionally pacifist, I also felt a great respect and gratitude for our military. I'm proud of our son-in-law and grandchildren who have served our country in this way.

Anyway, Mim loved me and accepted me in spite of my issues! We were on a date at the Farm Show in West Lampeter, Pennsylvania, when I asked her to marry me. We looked at cows and farm equipment and ate some ice cream and then I just popped the question! I know it wasn't very romantic, but it worked. She said yes!

We got married the next spring, April 5, 1947, at 11:00 A.M. in her parents' farmhouse. Mim remembers feeling so special as the neighbors came early that morning to prepare the dinner for our wedding day. They served a full course dinner for about 100

Jim and Mim's Wedding Day

our Wedding day

The morning of our wedding day was cloudy with just a little rain. About 10:00 it cleared off into a beautiful day. Shortly after 7:30 the cooks, consisting mostly of neighbors, arrived and soon there was the wonderful sound of friendly hurrying about setting tables, preparing food, arranging flowers, etc.

Finally 11:00 came, the hour we had so happily awaited. The trio began singing and -- we were married. Truly, it was the happiest moment of our life. After the delicious dinner we went to Lancaster to have our pictures taken while the second tables of guests were being served. Then there was the happy afternoon, filled with handshakes and best wishes from loved ones, admiring the beautiful gifts, and laughingly posing for snapshots. How wonderful it is to know that God has pronounced us husband and wife and that we will go thru life together.

About 4 o'clock amid farewells, and a due amount of confetti, crepe paper and tin cans, we left for our 2 wks. honeymoon. It was a perfect day.

Mim's diary description of their wedding day

people—which necessitated two seatings in the Hershey home. Two weeks later my parents had a similar dinner in our home for more of our relatives. Both of us are from large extended families.

At that time the Mennonite church did not approve of wearing jewelry, so we didn't give each other wedding bands. My gift to Mim? A very practical sewing machine! She still has it and it still works.

When we set off on our honeymoon, we had $250.00 and a two-door red Dodge that I was very proud of—the first car I bought that was not used. We thought we wanted to go to Florida so we headed south, but that's the closest we came to having travel plans. We had no reservations anywhere and neither of us had ever stayed in a motel before. I remember our first stop was a little cabin near Baltimore that had linoleum on the floors.

We made it to Florida, and one day we stopped at a touristy reptile farm. The establishment also had a game of chance, a big spinning wheel where patrons paid for a number and the wheel was spun to determine if your number was a winner. Well, we tried the wheel and we didn't win. The man at the wheel said we should try again and we'd surely win. We tried and of course lost again. We spent more money than we should have—I think we lost $30. This unsuccessful gambling venture caused us to be short of money for the rest of our trip. We went home by way of Sterling, Illinois, where I had relatives I thought we could stay with. I borrowed $25 from them so we could return to our home in Willow Street.

Wedding Gift

*The "honeymoon suite"!
A little cabin near Baltimore*

The red Dodge on the beach, Daytona, FL – on Jim and Mim's honeymoon

࿔

Wealth from gambling quickly disappears;
wealth from hard work grows.
Proverbs 13:11

࿔

Though the reptile farm story is not something I'm proud of, and I certainly do not espouse gambling, I do think it makes a point that I have a certain tolerance for taking risks. I don't know if that's something you're born with, but most entrepreneurs I know have had to be willing to take a risk of some kind—hopefully with much more common sense than I had at the reptile farm!—in order to get a business started. My loan from Mr. Wenger was of course the greater risk, because it involved our livelihood.

As I look back, I think you have to have a certain optimism that you can accomplish what you set out to do—maybe more so than sometimes seems realistic to most people. Of greatest value to me was that I have a supportive life partner. Mim has always been like a trooper about hanging in there with me, through good risks and bad—and I'll tell you about some of those later in the book.

Business Principles

If you want to create a business you have to be on the lookout for an opportunity. It doesn't usually just come to you—you have to be willing to make the effort to look for it.

Be willing to ask for help. Think about the people you know—is there anyone who could give you that leg up you need? If someone knows you are looking for a start, they may be willing to give you a hand.

Don't let a lack of resources keep you from your dream. Explore all the options available to you.

∽o∾

The diligent man makes good use of everything he finds.
Proverbs 12:27b

In 2011 Jim and Mim stand beside a replica of a 1936 Dodge panel truck, like the one he purchased with Verna's Potato Chips in 1946.

Sketch of Herr's first location.
"Verna's" in Lancaster (Charlotte Street) 1946

Tobacco Shed on Herr Farm 1947

West Willow Bakery 1949

Chapter 3

EARLY DAYS OF HERR'S

The final years of World War II were not an optimal time to begin a food company. Gas had been rationed, along with sugar and other commodities during the war. However, both Mim and I had learned from growing up in the Depression that it is possible to survive in hard times. Neither of us was afraid of hard work, and we were committed to the farm-family philosophy of "pulling together" to make something work. So with our newly-wed optimism we set to work.

❦

Hard work brings prosperity;
playing around brings poverty.
Proverbs 28:19

❦

Shortly after I purchased the business I changed the name to Herr's Potato Chips. I didn't want someone else's name on the bag, especially Verna's—I didn't even know who she was!

I would begin my day by peeling, slicing, and cooking the potato chips. I had one employee, Mrs. Armstrong (I don't remember her first name), who helped me half a day. During the afternoon, we would pack the chips into pound-size cans, half-pound cans, and five-cent bags. Before we were married, when Mim was still working for Mr. Wenger, I'd pick her up after her workday at the law firm and together we would finish packaging the chips, put them in the panel truck, and drive through Lancaster to sell them door-to-door. I went to Cabbage Hill and then down on Duke and Lime streets. Early on, we were bringing in $36.00 a week in sales.

Later I decided to move the business from Charlotte Street in Lancaster to the town of Willow Street, where my family's farm was located (by that time it was owned by my older brother). There was a vacant tobacco shed on the property that I thought would be the right size for making the potato chips. My brother agreed to rent it to me for our operation.

After we got married Mim worked full time with me and we rented an "apartment" in the Herr family farmhouse for $25.00 a month. We had three large rooms—one upstairs and two downstairs. The accommodations were sparse and didn't include indoor plumbing, but it was just down the lane from the tobacco shed, so we had no commute!

We worked long hours, often beginning the work day at 4:00 A.M. and not finishing until 11:00 P.M. We had learned from growing up on farms that long days are often necessary when there is work to be done. You don't think about it or question it—you just do what needs to be done. In our case, we needed to have the chips made and ready to sell by the afternoon, and in the evening we needed to have the potatoes and oil ready to make chips again the next morning.

Herr Family Farmhouse
Jim and Mim lived in several rooms in the back in their early marriage.

Sometimes in the evening we would drive 40 miles west to Hanover, Pennsylvania, to take chips to a distributor who was paying us 35 cents for a dozen five-cent bags. He would then take the chips to New York and sell them for 45 or 50 cents; he didn't make much money and the venture did not last.

Other evenings we would have to drive an hour or so south to the Baltimore Harbor to purchase potatoes for the next day. I usually bought potatoes from a local grower, but when local potatoes weren't available, we needed the ones from Florida that were shipped to Baltimore. It was often because of these trips that we were up late at night, trying to get ready for the next morning's work. Mim also did all the bookwork in the evenings.

Eventually I got tired of selling chips to individuals door-to-door. It was a hassle to find people at home, especially the customers who owed me money! I remember one lady in particular, who was never "available" to pay me, yet she always had her radio blaring and the lights on—I knew she was inside. At one point she owed me $5.00. I decided I didn't want to spend my time collecting money, so I looked into what it would take to sell to stores instead of individuals.

I didn't have a clue what to charge the stores, but I did some research on what competitors were charging and just went with that. I don't remember the first store that became a customer, but early on I sold some chips to a drugstore. The day before Christmas the gentleman who ran the drugstore asked me if I wanted a drink to celebrate the season. I thought he meant a Coke, so I said OK. He gave me some whiskey and it burned all the way down my throat. Then he offered me a chaser, but I didn't know what that was so I said, "No, I think I'll leave well enough alone!"

I loved selling (here was my chance to talk to people) and gradually I added additional stores to the route and our business expanded. Though we had stiff competition from other potato chip companies operating in the Lancaster area, we were growing too.

After two years on my brother's farm, I realized we were outgrowing our space. I looked around for a facility and found a 3,600-square-foot bakery located nearby in West Willow. The owners had stopped baking bread and the building was vacant. We rented the bakery as well as an adjacent house for our residence.

I called the landlord shortly after we moved there to ask if we could take in another boarder. He reminded me that the lease only allowed two. Then I announced that we had a new baby girl, and of course he was delighted. Miriam June (we call her June) was born in 1949, and two years later our son James Melvin, now known as J.M., was born.

We had added several full-time employees before moving to the bakery. The first employees hired at the farm were relatives and neighbors. We didn't advertise in newspapers or formally interview people. We just gave people a chance and if someone wasn't working as expected, we encouraged them to find another job.

When we needed additional help, we usually looked to our circle of friends. Dave Huber, a schoolmate of mine who had grown up on the farm next to ours, opened a public accounting service in Willow Street. When we were located at the bakery in West Willow, I hired his company to do our accounting, and he personally kept our books for nearly twenty years, even after we moved out of the area.

I hired my best friend, Harold Groff, along with Charlie Myers, to work in sales. As the business with stores increased, we hired two more salesmen: One was a salesman for a milk company, Art Herman, and the other was another good friend, Ben Fenninger.

I actually met Ben when I was dating Mim, because he was living in an apartment on Mim's dad's farm and working part time on the farm. He was also working for Armstrong Industries in Lancaster. When I was looking for additional sales people, I thought of Ben and offered him a job at a salary of $65 a week, but he told me he couldn't leave Armstrong for that money. Later, he developed a skin rash from the working conditions at Armstrong (he was allergic to something in the plant) and when I asked him another time if he

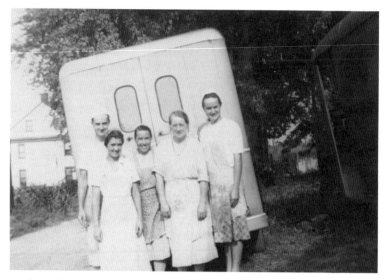

Left to Right: Jim, Mim, Employee Mary Pickel, Jim's Mother, Jim's sister Mary, 1947

wanted to work in sales for us, he accepted. I think we increased the offer by $5 or $10 a week.

Ben is a "people person" and I knew he would be a good salesman. I remember early in his employment we were working together on a sales route in Coatesville. The early trucks didn't have passenger seats so I sat on a potato chip can. The truck had a manual transmission and Ben wasn't used to shifting gears. We were stopped at a red light and when the light turned green he put the truck in gear and took off—and so did I! I flew off the potato chip can into the back of the truck. Ben was sure that would be his last day on the job, but he was a loyal employee for many years.

The truck Ben was driving was one of the pair of step-vans I purchased new in 1949. One was a Studebaker and the other was a Chevrolet. We needed the trucks to cover routes that expanded from Lancaster to include West Chester and Coatesville, as well as Wilmington, Delaware.

Ben became the first salesman to be paid on commission. His route was returning less than $700 in sales and we paid him a flat ten percent commission on sales. When I told him I wanted the routes to return $1,000 a week, Ben didn't tell me he thought I was crazy but I knew he thought it. When he was the first salesman to hit $1,000 on a route, I reminded him, "I told you that you would." Ben eventually became our first sales manager and Art Herman served as our first credit manager.

In those early years we terminated very few people. We fired one person for being dishonest (a customer reported him). Another salesman was dishonest but we didn't know about the theft at first. One day the man told his wife that after he was dead she was to tell us that he owed us money. She told him to go and tell us immediately. He sweated it out but he did it.

About this time I decided that cooking the potato chips was not the best use of my time, so I hired Lewis Gehman to take over the task. Lew had learned many of his skills by cooking doughnuts for soldiers in the United States Army. He had the foresight to see ways in which we could operate more efficiently, and he was good at fixing problems. When he took over the cooking, I went on the road to sell and build routes. After the routes were developed, I would turn them over to salesmen to maintain.

Jim & Mim responded affirmatively to an invitation to "help with the work" at a new mission church near Oxford. (The mission was started by the church they attended, Willow Street Mennonite Church.)

Lew became our production manager and worked faithfully with me until his retirement in 1984. With help from some of our suppliers, I learned about new and better cooking processes. We constructed a new kettle measuring three feet by five feet and had burners installed. At first we used lard in the kettle, but we switched to corn oil due to our customers' preferences. That was a big decision, as Herr's became known as a "lighter" chip. Today we offer a product called "Old Fashioned," a lard-cooked chip that is manufactured for us, but throughout most of our history our products have been fried in vegetable oil.

As I learned the business, I began to enjoy having my own company, and as I began to network with others in the industry I started to appreciate the snack food business. Two years after I had borrowed the money from Mr. Wenger I paid back my loan, and I was glad I had stuck it out.

It helped that because of what Mim had learned at Lancaster Business College she could take care of the accounting. As we worked together, God was working things out for us, just as He promised in Psalm 37:4.

As I saw the Lord's goodness in keeping His promise to give me the desires of my heart, I also began to learn what the verse means about "delighting yourself in Him." Mim and I were asked to help teach at a small mission church, located near Oxford, Pennsylvania. It was a 25-mile drive from our home in West Willow, and, though it was a stretch to drive that far several times a week, helping to get that little church started was one way we could delight ourselves in serving Him.

Business Principles

Be willing to work hard to make something "go." Don't think
so much about how long the hours are or that others are not
working as hard as you are. Be committed to your own goal and
stick to it.

If you are married, be sure you "pull together" at your work.
Even if your spouse is not working in the business, it takes
commitment from both of you, because there are going to be
times when you get too discouraged or tired to keep going if
you don't have that support from each other.

Don't give up too quickly. At first I thought I had made a wrong
decision about making potato chips, but as I stuck with it I
learned to appreciate the business.

Chapter 4

FIRE!

The afternoon of September 5, 1951, I was selling chips in Wilmington, Delaware, and my time was getting away from me. I knew we had some folks coming to the house that evening for a prayer meeting and it was already 5:30. I called Mim and told her I'd be late—to go ahead and eat and give the kids their evening baths without me, because I'd barely make it home in time for the meeting.

As Mim was giving June her bath on the second floor of our home, she glanced out the window and spotted flames coming from the potato chip plant (we still called it the bakery). The workday had concluded, the employees had left for the day, and none of the equipment was operating. Cooking oil had dripped onto a hot fire brick and burst into flames.

Within minutes the building was fully engulfed in fire. Our home and the bakery building were separated by only twelve feet.

"I was looking outside towards the old bake shop," Mim recalls. "I can still see those flames licking the white-framed building. I scooped up June, wrapped her in a towel, and called the local fire company. By that time, the fire was roaring and the old frame building was pretty

Mim with J.M. and June

much gone. J.M., our six-month-old baby, was asleep in a carriage and I took June and him outside. Figuring our house would burn along with the bakery, I made sure I had a pacifier and went to the neighbor's, our landlord Ted Bowers. I sat on the bank in their yard with my children and just watched the bakery burn."

Mim recalls passersby stopping to offer aid as the fire trucks arrived. A couple of sailors were on their way to the Bainbridge Naval Training Center, and they went into the house and carried out the furniture. We had only furnished a few rooms, so there wasn't much, except for a "treasure" we had—our baby grand piano, which was a gift from Mim's father (he made sure each of his married children had a piano in their home). The sailors quickly carried it outside and put it in a nearby field.

I was oblivious to it all, just trying to make it home in time for the prayer meeting. When I got closer to our place, I began to see fire trucks and bedlam. There were lots of cars along the road, and they seemed to be in front of where we lived. Imagine my panic when I realized that it was my family and my business that were in jeopardy! When I saw Mim and the kids on our neighbor's lawn, I was so relieved they were safe.

I immediately knew that the building was a total loss. It was a combustible building and it had been leveled in a hurry. The fire was so hot that we could see blistered paint on the bathroom door where Mim had been bathing June, but no other damage had taken place to the house, because some of the firemen had gone to the roof and sprayed it with water to keep the fire from destroying it.

All four of our parents arrived at the scene to help us. Mim's father secured hamburgers for the firemen. The furniture was carried back into the home, but when we went to take the piano back in, there was no way it would fit through the door without taking the legs off. We still don't know how those sailors got the piano out. Mim and I stayed in our home that night but the children stayed with my parents until we could re-group.

What a confusing time that was! We had been engrossed in making and selling potato chips and then all of a sudden, there was a 180-degree shift—everything was gone!

Salesman Ben Fenninger had loaded his truck the afternoon before. The day following the fire, when he was delivering Herr's chips in Coatesville, a delivery milkman saw him and asked, "What are you doing here?" Ben didn't know what he meant, and the guy told him the plant had burned. Ben said, "No, it didn't." The milkman then pulled out a copy of a newspaper with a story on the fire. He called me right away and I had to admit that in my confusion I hadn't even let him know what had happened.

∽∘∾

We can make our plans,
but the final outcome is in God's hands.
Proverbs 16:1

∽∘∾

The insurance man came to our home the next day and offered us $4,000 for the loss of the business. This was taking into account that our trucks did not burn because they were on the road, and our car was fine.

Mim and I discussed whether we should rebuild or do something different. We had to make a quick decision, because if we were not going to continue the business, we would have to tell our customers (not to mention our employees) that the business was closing. If we were going to continue, we'd have to somehow get chips to our customers until we could rebuild.

It was a decision that would influence the rest of our lives, but it didn't take us long to make. We would keep going. I'm not sure what other options we had, except I thought I could possibly work on my brother's farm. But by now we had five years of experience in business, a base of customers, and employees we enjoyed working with. I also had learned to know some people in the industry who I felt might help us.

One of those was Si Musser, owner of Charles Chips, and he graciously responded to our need. Si knew that if they were in trouble we would help them. I also knew the Utz family; both companies agreed to sell us bulk chips in big cans, from which we scooped out chips to fill our bags. It was the best we could do. We had to take care of our customers.

We were so grateful to my father for offering us the use of his two-car garage in Willow Street as a base to pack the chips to keep the business operating, but of course that was a short-term solution. We began searching for another location to manufacture Herr's chips.

The search included the area around Oxford, Pennsylvania. We were traveling in that direction because of our work at Mount Vernon Mennonite Church. Mim and I felt a lot of loyalty to that little church, and to be located closer would mean we could be of greater help there. We knew it would mean it would be less convenient to visit our parents and siblings, but we both had the desire to give our extra time to the church. We learned that there was a plot of 13 acres available in the town of Oxford, so we seriously considered buying that for our new location.

Now it happened that John and Miriam Thomas, another young couple who were helping with the mission church at Mount Vernon, learned of a house with some property in Nottingham (just three miles from Oxford) that they brought to our attention. Through the years our paths have crossed with the Thomases' many times (John and most of their children have worked at Herr's, we worked on many church projects together, and their youngest son is married to our youngest daughter), but perhaps the most far-reaching comment John ever made to me was to recommend that we take a look at this house.

We learned that the property on which the house was located included 45 acres and not only the house but also an old barn. We were impressed with the property and we liked the house, but the asking price was $20,000, an amount we just couldn't come up with.

We believed the Lord would lead us to the right spot, so we prayed and somehow felt the Nottingham land was the way we should go. Eventually the owners agreed to sell us 37 acres for $18,000. We can see now that it's good we didn't buy the site in Oxford, because we didn't realize how much the business would grow and 13 acres wouldn't have accommodated our growth.

*In everything you do, put God first, and he will direct
you and crown your efforts with success.*
Proverbs 3:6

The property we purchased is the current site of our Nottingham plant. Later, we purchased an additional 13 acres, the location of our corporate offices. Throughout our 65 years we have acquired additional acreage, much of which we now irrigate with the water we use in processing potatoes.

Financing for the purchase and rebuilding of the plant came from small loans from family members and a loan from a local bank. Both my parents and Mim's parents loaned us $5,000, money that we quickly repaid. Family and friends helped by tearing down the barn on the property and re-using the timber in the new 4,500-square-foot factory we constructed at a cost of $11,000.

My uncle Clarence Herr, who was helping in the rebuilding, suggested the new plant should be constructed in the middle of the property. We didn't take his advice, but years later, when we needed additional space, the plant was moved to the center of the property—exactly where he said it should go in the first place!

Money was scarce, but we believed we made a good purchase. Someone from Rising Sun, Maryland, later offered us $20,000 for the house alone. I'm glad we didn't take the offer. We kept the home, renting out the top floor and living on the first floor. We paid the $80.00-a-month mortgage with the rent. This is the house we live in today (both floors!).

Business Principles

Sometimes the unforeseen happens, and you just can't make it without the help of others. Don't be too proud to ask for help. We could never have made it through this period if we had tried to do everything on our own. Be willing to acknowledge the help of others and the help of the Lord to get you through the tough times. A business requires more than any one person or family can offer.

When people offer you advice, listen carefully but then make your own decisions. We made some that were right and some that weren't, but in the end you have to make the decision and accept the responsibility for it.

✺

The wise man is glad to be instructed,
but a self-sufficient fool falls flat on his face.
Proverbs 10:8

The house on the 37-acre Nottingham property, 1952

Chapter 5

REBUILDING AND GROWTH IN NOTTINGHAM

While the cost of rebuilding was covered by loans, I had no money for working capital to begin production. I tried my local banker but money was tight and he decided their bank had loaned me as much as they were willing. I had already asked my family and friends for so much help, I didn't want to ask for more. I didn't know where to turn.

One of the construction workers building the plant mentioned to me that he personally knew a banker in Newark, Delaware, and he thought he might be willing to loan me some money. Leaving no stone unturned, I headed to Newark. Sure enough, after listening to my impassioned plea for help, Mr. Matthews issued me a bank loan for $1,500.00. That boosted my spirits enough that I decided to make one more purchase before we began our Nottingham operation.

You are a poor specimen if you can't stand
the pressure of adversity.
Proverbs 24:10

I had not used the insurance money for the construction of the plant because I had felt it was important to start in our new facility with a different type of cooker to allow us greater production capacity. I learned that there was a used automatic cooker for sale in Boston that could process 100 pounds of chips an hour (the old iron kettle we had used in the West Willow bakery could process a maximum of 40 pounds an hour). I knew this could make a huge difference to our company. So after I had gotten the vote of confidence from the Newark banker, I headed to Boston to purchase the new cooker.

By the spring of 1952—just six months after the fire—we were back in operation. Several of our key employees from West Willow decided to stay with our company and drive the distance to Nottingham each day. I feel it was their loyalty and hard work that were vital to our company's ability to transition to a new level of growth. My parents drove to Nottingham every day to help us, and picked up Mary Mowrer, an early employee, on the way.

Jim's father operating the potato peeler, spring 1952

Nottingham—how we have grown to love this town! The first Christmas we were here, I took a can of chips and a Christmas greeting to each of our neighbors; it was the beginning of many decades of good relationships with them. In fact, recently we went to the funeral of the last of our generation to live in our section of Nottingham, a poignant reminder of how time moves along!

One young teenager I met that first Christmas, John Featherman, lived with his parents just two doors away from us, and as we talked he agreed to work for the company at odd jobs if we had a special need. For example, one day we asked him to go to Baltimore and purchase salt, because we were nearly out—that kind of thing. Over the course of time, we developed a special friendship with this young man, keeping up with him as he went off to Penn State, then the United States Navy, then law school. John went on to become a very successful Chester County attorney, often representing Herr's in legal matters.

As the business grew, we were always interested in buying neighboring properties, and often John would handle the legal work for us. Early on we were involved in a transaction where the seller grew quite unreasonable and John was frustrated about it. I remember telling John that it was okay, that if both parties don't feel like they're being treated fairly, the deal shouldn't take place anyway. If you take advantage of someone, I reminded him, your reputation will be tarnished and you won't be able to make the next deal. He later told me that he learned a lesson that day in treating others with respect (even if they are contentious).

Trucks at loading dock, 1956

I treasure our relationship with people like John—we have a history together. I like to do business locally as much as I can, giving support to the community from which we draw so much benefit. Those early years were years of rapid expansion, and Nottingham was the epicenter.

It wasn't just Herr's that was expanding, though—the whole snack food industry exploded in the 1950s. It was the post-War boom and people were moving from rural to urban settings, from farming to manufacturing. More leisure time was available and television was introduced into people's homes. Americans began to look forward to snacking while they watched their favorite TV shows, and as the customer base increased so did advertising on television. Some of the major companies began to advertise salty snacks on TV, and it helped increase consumer awareness for the whole industry.

We advertised on the radio that our chips were "lively, light, and delicious," and they really were. Our market share grew, especially with Acme markets in the 1960s and 1970s in the Philadelphia region. Our salesmen used to say that they could open a bag of chips, and the chips would sell themselves.

But it was not a time for resting on our laurels. As the snack food industry grew, we needed to keep abreast of it all. I think it's important to keep informed about what others are doing in your line of work, to see what you can learn in order to give yourself a leg up. We didn't innovate just to be the first to do something, but we were pretty quick to take advantage of new ways of doing things. I found that using up-to-date equipment soon paid for itself.

Packaging equipment was one innovation that we took advantage of. You can lose lots of money if the bags consistently have more than the weight listed on the bag, and of course the law requires that they can't have less. So weights are a big deal in manufacturing, and today, 60 years later, we are using equipment so advanced that the weights of our packages are accurate to the weight of one chip. But in the beginning, someone used to have to scoop the chips into a bag, put the bag on the scale, and then individually adjust the weight of each bag. You can imagine how much time that took, and how getting better equipment could improve that process.

I purchased up-to-date packaging equipment early on. The Woodman Company had developed an Air-Weigh System that consisted of a bin (to hold the freshly cooked chips) in the center of a rotating system of chutes like spokes around the hub of a wheel.

The chutes had doors that allowed just the right weight of chips to fall into a bag at the end of the chute. After the bag was filled with chips, someone had to remove the bag and run it through the heat sealer, then place it in a box on a cart. Once it was full, the cart was then rolled to the nearby dock for the salesmen to pick up.

Meanwhile, the chutes kept turning, and someone had to be ready on the other side to put bags on the chutes for the chips to fall into. You couldn't be dozing off on that job, or there'd be chips all over the floor. Actually, Mim became one of the best operators of that machine. She did that, or she worked on the accounting, while June and J.M. took their naps, each in a seat of our car parked at the loading dock. She was a great multi-tasker! She has always been the most organized person I know.

Mim and Mary Mowrer packing chips

Cans of chips had to be dumped into packaging equipment.

I should also explain how the chips got into the bin to be packed. There was a big can at the end of the cooker, collecting all the newly fried chips, and when it got full a person had to carry it over to the packing equipment, go up some stairs, and dump it into the bin. Now, with all of our conveyer belts and automation, it's hard to remember that people used to have to actually carry the product from one step to the next.

Lew Gehman, our production manager, was busy running the cooker and then filling the packers, and I could soon see that he had to have help. One of our applicants was Harold Blank, a young man just out of high school who had grown up on a nearby farm. I thought about the work ethic required on a farm, and I knew he would understand the mentality that says, "You just do whatever has to be done, and don't worry about a job description." So we hired him to help Lew.

Harold began working at Herr's in 1960 by carrying chips from the cooker to the packer; he then progressed to operating the automatic potato peeler. Later Harold began running the cooker and was named production manager when Lew retired; eventually he was made Senior Vice President of Manufacturing. He was responsible for our many plant expansions and the equipment layout over the years. He retired in 2009, after 49 years of "doing what had to be done."

Harold has been successful at a great diversity of positions for us, just like many of our long-term employees. I like to see people develop and expand their own personal horizons, as well as those of the company. If there is a new position open, rather than always hiring someone new, I like to give the current employees a chance to learn and grow.

One of the people Harold brought on to help with production was another local farm-boy, Dan Jackson. Dan started with Herr's in sales, then became a key long-term production manager at Herr's.

Another key employee in those early years in Nottingham was Charles Temple. He was the kind of engineer who could fix anything. As we grew and got more equipment, we needed him to figure out how to make it all work. He came up with new ideas for conveying the chips from one piece of equipment to another, as well as a monorail system to take packed cases to the warehouse. He also set up the truck garage and maintenance shop. When I think of what people like Lew, Harold, and Charles offered our company, I'm reminded that I hired a lot of people who knew more than I did about their work. You have to rely on the knowledge of others and let them take a project and run with it.

∾o∾

Plans go wrong with too few counselors;
many counselors bring success.
Proverbs 15:22

∾o∾

Our truck routes expanded two or three at a time, and salesmen and additional trucks were added when needed. As I've said, the salesmen supplied the Herr's products directly to the stores through our Direct Store Delivery (DSD) system, a valuable asset of Herr Foods today. This is a relatively expensive method of distributing our products, but it guarantees store managers that every package is fresh. And we've always been blessed with good salesmen through the years.

Mim and I were still very active in the Mount Vernon Mennonite Church, and our pastor's oldest son eventually became a 45-year employee. Jim Kreider was a teenager in the Sunday School class we taught, and when he was a junior in high school I asked him to go with me on a sales call to York, Pennsylvania. I always liked him and thought he'd be a good worker, so when he graduated from high school I hired him to work at the plant. Sure enough, he turned out to be the kind of person who knew how to work hard and was willing to do whatever he was asked.

I think Jim's first job was unloading potatoes. At that time we got potatoes in 100-pound bags and they had to be unloaded from trucks, cut open, and dumped into the potato peeler. It was a tough job, but there was hardly anyone who didn't help with that job from time to time, including Mim! Just like on the farm, we did whatever had to be done whether it was in our "job description" or not! After Jim got married, he and his wife Rozie even came and stayed with our children when Mim and I would go to conventions.

∽o∾

*A faithful employee is as refreshing
as a cool day in the hot summertime.*
Proverbs 25:13

∽o∾

Mim and I started attending snack food industry meetings as early as the late 1940s. Our first national convention was in Ohio, and there were so many chippers there we all decided to form regional meetings. After about five years I was asked to become involved in the governing body and eventually became chairman of the Eastern Region. There I grew to know my competitors and we could talk about common problems and concerns. We discussed potato crops and what was new in the industry. Sometimes, it was kind of funny the game of bluff we played, as we sought each other's advice but didn't want to be too helpful to each other!

But I don't think we have ever had a competitor that we couldn't talk to and be friendly with. Of course, each is interested in growing his own company, so we would fight for sales, but we all understood that and still got along well personally.

Eventually (in 1979) I became president of the national organization, known then as the Potato Chip Institute and now as the Snack Food Association, which opened my eyes to the role that our United States government plays in our business environment. In fact, I think that subject is worth a chapter of its own.

Business Principles

Money is your tool for operation, and sometimes your most pressing job as a businessperson is to find the resources that will allow your business to thrive. Don't give up easily—if you are passionate about what you are doing, you may find someone who will believe in you enough to give you the loan you need to take the next step. Be persistent and try to stay optimistic.

Become connected with people in your industry and learn all you can from them. Try to stay abreast of new ways of doing things and don't be afraid of change.

Be open to giving employees opportunities to diversify in their career paths. If a new position is needed, perhaps someone you already employ would be energized by the challenge of learning something new.

Chapter 6

AN APPRECIATION FOR OUR COUNTRY

∽o∾

Godliness exalts a nation,
but sin is a reproach to any people.

Proverbs 14:34

∽o∾

Most of us don't know what it's like to be restricted from practicing our beliefs or from pursuing our careers. I hope it always stays like that in America.

This wasn't the case for my family in earlier generations. The Herr family migrated from Switzerland to Germany in the seventeenth century because of religious persecution. The Catholic Church called them heretics (for their belief in only adult baptism) and the Protestants called them law-breakers (for their refusal to go to war). But they had a reputation as good farmers and hard workers, so they were invited to go and help rebuild an area of Germany that had been severely damaged by the Thirty Years' War.

Settling in Germany, where the ravages of war had burned the buildings and left the land overgrown with brush, was challenging enough, but soon another war broke out. Faced with more persecution and ever-increasing taxes, in 1710 a group of Mennonites decided to risk the hazardous voyage to America, where they had heard there was land and freedom available.

The way they settled in Pennsylvania was that William Penn, who had converted to the Quaker faith (similar to that of the Mennonites in many ways), experienced religious persecution and he wanted to protect others who suffered for their faith. He granted a settlement in what is now Lancaster County to nine Mennonite men in the early eighteenth century.

The oldest building that is still standing from that early settlement is a house that was built in 1719 by one of my ancestors, Hans Herr, a bishop in the Mennonite church. (That house has been restored to its colonial-era appearance and is now a museum in Lancaster County.) The new settlers used their farming skills and work ethic to develop the area where I grew up; in fact our farm was less than a mile away from the Hans Herr house.

Photo Courtesy of 1719 Hans Herr House and Museum

1719 Hans Herr House

As I was growing up, though, I didn't know anything about Hans Herr or the persecution that had driven my ancestors to Pennsylvania. I knew we Mennonites were different from the general culture, but we didn't suffer any persecution or even prejudice that I can remember. We were enough of a sub-culture that in our day-to-day lives on our farms we were mostly surrounded by people like us.

As I got into business, my perspective began to change. I began to interact with people from other areas of our country and with Christians of other denominations, and I realized that there are other ways to look at things. Over the years I've become more ecumenical and less separatist than some in my denomination.

Though as a young man I didn't even vote, as I became more involved in the snack food industry, I became very interested in politics and in protecting the business environment from government legislation that would hurt someone's chances of starting a small business. I knew that I had been blessed to experience the wonderful freedom we have in this country and I wanted to be sure it would be there for others.

At the time we began the business, we simply hired the people we wanted to hire, we paid them what we could afford to pay them, we bought and sold supplies at the best prices, and we created our own working environment. As I saw more and more legislation being introduced that would restrict business, I wanted to become involved. Sometimes politicians don't realize the adverse effect their well-intentioned laws can have on people's freedom to start small. This has a ripple effect through the economy, because if you discourage small business you take away a lot of jobs those businesses

Jim discusses small business issues with President George Bush during a national leadership conference in Washington, D.C.

could have created. After all, small businesses create the majority of new jobs and employ the most people in our country.

Through my work in the Snack Food Association, I learned of an organization called the National Federation of Independent Business (NFIB). The NFIB is a non-profit, non-partisan organization that was founded in 1943, and it is considered the guardian of, and advocate for, small and independent businesses. The organization educates members on both economic and political issues, and it seeks to guard our free enterprise system.

I became a member of NFIB in 1955, and I've been a member ever since. In 1972 I was asked to become a member of the Board of Directors, and in 1991 I became the chairman, a position I held at the time of the sudden death of our NFIB president, John Sloan. The Board asked me to replace him, and I agreed that I would serve as president and CEO for six months until they could find a replacement. I knew I should stay focused on Herr's, though during this period I learned how capable and responsible our employees were; they kept the business strong in my frequent absences.

During those six months that I was NFIB's president, in January, 1992, it happened that President George H. W. Bush decided to take a group of U.S. businessmen to the Far East on a 12-day trade mission. One of the people on their invitation list was the president of NFIB, so there I was! I happened to be at the right spot at the right time. It was one of the greatest honors I've experienced—to ride in Air Force One and to interact with people like the presidents of

Business leaders accompany Bush

These business leaders will be with President Bush at various times during his trip to Asia:

Dexter Baker, Air Products and Chemicals Inc.
Winston Chen, Solectron Corp.
Beverly Dolan, Textron Inc.
Robert Galvin, Motorola Inc.
Joseph Gorman, TRW Inc.
Maurice Greenberg, American International Corp.
Bronce Henderson, Detroit Center Tool
James Herr, Herr Foods Inc.
Lee Iacocca, Chrysler Corp.
Robert Maricich, American of Martinsville
Raymond Marlow, Marlow Industries
John Marous, Westinghouse Electric Corp.
Harold Poling, Ford Motor Co.
Heinz Prechter, ASC Inc.
John Reilly, Tenneco Automotive
James Robinson III, American Express
David Roderick, USX Corp.
C.J. Silas, Phillips Petroleum Co.
Robert Stempel, GM Corp.
Michael von Clemm, Merrill Lynch & Co.
Patrick Ward, Caltex Petroleum Corp.

From USA Today, 12/30/91

the big three auto manufacturers and other large firms. We went to Australia, Singapore, South Korea, and Japan.

I've had the honor of meeting other U.S. presidents too, and mostly that's because of either NFIB or the Snack Food Association. You may wonder what this has to do with building a business, but I am always energized by being around people who are more influential and more knowledgeable than I am. Also, you never know when you can be a blessing to someone, even if you think they are "above" you.

During the time I was working a lot in the NFIB Washington office I got invited to various business events, and one stands out in my memory. You may remember that in 1991, Russia was big in business news because the Soviet Union had recently collapsed and Russia was transitioning from a government-controlled economy to a private enterprise system. When President Boris Yeltsin was in Washington, I was invited to spend a few minutes with him, representing NFIB. I got to communicate with him my belief that small business is the backbone of a healthy modern economy, and that whatever he could do to promote entrepreneurship would help Russia.

∽∾∾

A friendly discussion is as stimulating as the sparks that fly when iron strikes iron.

Proverbs 27:17

∽∾∾

It's disappointing that there was so much corruption in Russia that small business people never really had a chance to thrive. It reinforced in my mind the need to keep our country a land of opportunity for the average citizen. I say all this to encourage you to use whatever opportunities you are given to help keep our country strong. You may think I'm naïve, but I take literally the verse in Proverbs 22:29 that says, "Do you know a hard-working man? He shall be successful and stand before kings!"

Herr advises Yeltsin

Promote growth, businessman urges

By CHRISTOPHER BIONDI
Staff Writer

WEST NOTTINGHAM — Jim Herr, chairman and chief executive officer of Herr Foods Inc., was among a dozen businessmen who met with Russian President Boris Yeltsin during this week's Washington summit.

Secretary of Commerce Barbara Franklin invited Herr to the meeting and to witness the signing of several accords by presidents Bush and Yeltsin, including one that aims to cut nuclear arsenals by two-thirds.

"It was certainly a momentous occasion because of the fact that instead of spending a lot of money fighting, we are spending it to get a free enterprise system working in Russia," said Herr in an interview.

Before the signing, Herr — also chairman of the National Federation of Independent Business — had an opportunity to discuss business with Yeltsin at a 45-minute meeting organized by the Commerce Department.

"I suggested to (Yeltsin) that if he wants to help the free enterprise system to grow, he needs to allow regulations and laws that would promote growth," said Herr.

"(Yeltin's) overall response to all of us was that they are working frantically trying to have laws enacted to make it possible for growth in the business world," he said.

Among Yeltsin's missions here was to urge Congress to pass a $24 billion aid package Bush has proposed.

"I think President Bush is suggesting a modest amount of help and is hoping that Congress will pass legislation to have that come about," said Herr. "I think it's the right thing to do. We can't go

See HERR, Page A8

From Daily Local News, 06/20/'92

I got hooked on the book of Proverbs in 1980, through the ministry of a person named Bill Gothard, who was holding conferences in many cities across the U.S. Several members of our family attended a session in Baltimore and Gothard challenged the 3,000 or so of us in the audience to read some of the Word of God every day. He suggested the book of Proverbs, because with its 31 chapters you can read one chapter per day. He said that we would find new thoughts each time we read it, and I found this to be true.

My personal favorite chapter is the eighth day of the month—chapter 8. In that chapter Wisdom says, "I give good advice and common sense." After reading that a few times, I asked God, "How can I take Wisdom along to work?" The very next day, in chapter 9, two verses stood out. Verses 10 and 11 say, "For the reverence and fear of God are basic to all wisdom. Knowing God results in every other kind of understanding. I, Wisdom, will make the hours of your day more profitable and the years of your life more fruitful." I began to see that by giving reverence to God, you are taking Wisdom to work.

I got an idea that we could tie the book of Proverbs into our leadership of Herr's as a source of strength to the company and to others. I began to strategize about how to include Proverbs in our business and the idea came to me that we could print and distribute copies to customers and friends as a gift from our company. Then I thought, "Who could be more helped by the wisdom in Proverbs than the leaders of our country?" so I began to dream of sending each person in Congress a copy.

I talked with Clair Leaman—a friend who had a graphic design and commercial printing firm—about the idea, and he agreed to help me. We contacted Tyndale House Publishers, the copyright holder for the *Living Psalms and Proverbs* and they gave us permission to print and bind our own copies. Clair came up with the idea of calling it "Chips of Wisdom." I wrote an introductory message encouraging readers to take its message to heart. To download the Chips of Wisdom, go to: herrs.com/chipsofwisdomapp or scan one of the QR codes for your electronic device.

We sent copies to President Reagan and his cabinet and to each member of Congress, and

iTunes

Google Play

we received 114 letters back from them. I prayed that this little book, that has so much truth in it, would help someone at some decision point in our government to look to God for wisdom. I believe that if the leaders of our country will look to God for wisdom, He will guide them as they create legislation, and our country can remain a land of opportunity for everyone.

Business Principles

Use whatever opportunities you have to be a blessing to others—wherever they are in your sphere of influence.

Work to promote a healthy free enterprise system in our country.

The good influence of godly citizens causes a city to prosper,
but the moral decay of the wicked drives it downhill.

Proverbs 11:11

Chapter 7

MOVING FORWARD

I've always felt that a company that stands still will eventually go backward. You always want to grow and expand your horizons.

Overall, the 1950s were a time of expansion for our industry and for Herr's, but we sure had some setbacks along the way. In the spring of 1952 there was a potato shortage, which if you think about it is devastating to a potato chip manufacturer! The price of potatoes spiked to three times their normal cost because of unfavorable weather conditions.

I talked with my friend Si Musser from Charles Chips and we agreed that I would borrow a truck and drive to North Carolina, where we would purchase potatoes at $7.00 a bag. I would buy 375 hundred-pound bags and we would split them. Well, by the time I got back to Pennsylvania, the price had dropped to $5.00 a bag, but Si kept his word and paid me the price we had agreed upon. We didn't have a written contract, and he could have backed out of our agreement, but he was a man of his word. This reinforced to me that one of the keys to long-term success is keeping your word.

I had a chance to put that into practice for myself a short while later. One August I had visited a Lancaster County potato grower, Morris Nissley, and agreed to purchase $10,000 worth of his crop. As soon as I returned home it began to rain and it rained for two weeks, causing the potatoes I had purchased to develop a jelly rot. I took them anyway and placed them in our plant's storage cellar with the idea that they were still usable. They weren't. We had to haul them out with a manure spreader.

∽o∾

The Lord demands fairness in every business deal.
He established this principle.
Proverbs 16:11

∽o∾

At the time I wasn't sure how I would get the $10,000 together to pay the farmer. I told him I could pay off the amount $1,000 a year from our profits. Within days a man in the lumber business randomly stopped by to say he wanted to purchase some of the trees on our land. He paid me several thousand dollars for them. Shortly after that, someone wanted to purchase a building lot, and before long I had the whole $10,000. We paid for the potatoes from the sale of assets I had not even considered.

∽o∾

Don't withhold repayment of your debts.
Don't say "some other time," if you can pay now.
Proverbs 3:27, 28

In October of 1954, Mother Nature dealt us another blow, with a deadly category 3 hurricane. The employees had gone home for the day and I was in the plant when the storm lifted a portion of our new roof and a steel column shifted and fell, knocking me against a concrete loading platform and breaking several ribs. Moments later, a piece of the steel column landed on my ankle and broke it. Terrified, I managed to crawl beside a cooker, the largest piece of equipment nearby, for protection.

Hurricane Hazel, 1954

When it was all over, I painfully limped across the yard to our home, which thankfully had withstood the strong winds. However, the building nearby that we used for a warehouse was completely flattened and many of our vehicles were destroyed.

∽०∾

Disaster strikes like a cyclone and the wicked are whirled away.
But the good man has a strong anchor.
Proverbs 10:25

∽०∾

The 1950s were full of blessings, too. Our second son, Edwin Hershey ("Ed"), was born April 19, 1955. With three young children at home, Mim's role in the business became more focused on being my confidante and supporter, rather than going to the plant or office each day. She has always been indispensable to me—giving good insights and wisdom whenever decisions need to be made, and always offering the listening ear in times of difficulty or dilemma.

Mim is also a very hospitable person, and since our home is adjacent to the plant, some of our key business associates would come over to the house for dinner with us in the evening. They didn't seem to mind the bedlam caused by our little children, or the simplicity of our meals. They knew we were genuinely glad to get to know them personally.

We began to plan parties at Christmas and in the summer for our employees and their spouses. We feel it's important for employees to enjoy interacting when they're not on the job too, and the company could provide some socials for them. Christmas soon outgrew our dining room table and we rented a room at a nearby restaurant. Eventually we began bringing in some sort of entertainment, such as a musical group or a comedian. The summer event, which we now call the "Summer Social," was always held in our backyard and it is still held on the campus of the business (close to our backyard). Everyone brings their children and we have tents set up with games and clowns and music in addition to the barbeque.

One of our major business decisions came up in 1958: Should we add seasoning to our chips? Today that seems like such a "given"—we have all kinds of new flavors and we advertise our product as a way to "live life with flavor." But back then, it was a new concept and we had to be careful. Would consumers get confused about what

"Summer Social" in Jim and Mim's backyard

"Herr's Potato Chips" were? Would they be willing to buy something different? Would it cut into our regular sales?

Our competitors began to try it, and we saw there was some consumer demand, so we began to produce a barbeque flavored potato chip. It became very successful, so we next developed a sour cream and onion chip. Our Old Bay™ seasoned chips were suggested by an employee, since that is a popular flavor in the Chesapeake Bay area. Another popular one was our Salt and Vinegar chip.

To this day we try new flavors. Some of them are winners; others get taken off the market. We try not to have so many products that a store's limited shelf space is overloaded. Ideas for seasoned chips are given to our Research and Development people, and we have a review system to test the flavors and develop new packaging for them. It's a real art to get the right mix of products on the shelf of a retail store.

Our family expanded as our third son, Herbert Eugene ("Gene") was born July 17, 1957, and our second daughter, Martha Jane, was born October 12, 1959. Our five children have all grown up in the business, so to speak. Living across the lawn from the factory, they interacted with the employees (probably to our embarrassment if we knew all that they said or did!), they worked at odd jobs such as sweeping out the truck bays in the evenings or mowing the lawn, and they worked in the plant itself as they became old enough. Our family didn't separate work from everyday living—it was all part of our daily lives, regardless of the time of day. Many business events or decisions were discussed at mealtime.

By 1961, we had 26 employees and a weekly payroll of $2,000. We had 10 routes that covered a radius of about 50 miles. Our mantra then was the same as it is today: to provide quality products at a competitive price and to back up the products with honesty, integrity, and dependable service.

By that time we had begun using our Direct Store Delivery (DSD) system to distribute other products along with the ones we manufactured. We wanted to be a full-service snack company, so that retailers would be less inclined to bring in other vendors who might also sell them chips. We sold salted nuts, dried meat sticks, pretzels, crackers, popcorn, cookies, and, on occasion, my mother's homemade chocolates.

Now there was a product that no one else could match! My mother, who was a good cook, decided to set up a small business of her own, on the top floor of their Willow Street garage (the same location that we had used after the fire). She specialized in making chocolate

Ira L. and Mary Stauffer Herr,
parents of James Stauffer Herr

Isaac and Esther Burkhart Hershey, parents of Miriam Esther Hershey

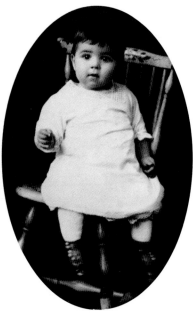

James Stauffer Herr
born August 6th, 1924

Miriam Esther Hershey
born November 29th, 1926

Young J.M. loading truck

The Herr children in 1959

Herr Family at the Greenbrier, summer of 2011, with 57 of the then 59 family members in attendance

Inducted into the Small Business Administration Hall of Fame, 2004

The NFIB honored Jim and Mim for many years of contributions to the free enterprise system. The plaque in the photo reads: "THE JIM & MIM HERR FREE ENTERPRISE CENTER. In recognition of Jim & Mim Herr's dedication to America's small businesses and to the free enterprise system."

Jim with Herr's truck, 1956

Jim with Herr's truck (same location), 1992

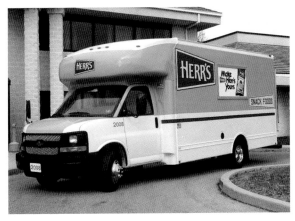

Newest Truck, 2012

SBA Names James S. Herr State Small Businessman Of The Year

James S. Herr of Nottingham, President of Herr's Potato Chips, Inc., has been named Pennsylvania's "Small Businessman of the Year".

Herr was honored Friday in an award ceremony held at The Red Fox Inn, near Kennett Square. Prior to the combined award ceremony and luncheon, a tour of the facilities of Herr's Potato Chips, Inc, was made by representatives of the Small Business Administration and officials representing Philadelphia area banks: First Pennsylvania, Central Penn National Bank, Philadelphia National Bank, Continental Bank and Trust Company, Industrial Valley Bank, The Fidelity Bank, Lincoln National Bank, Frankford Trust and Delaware County National Bank.

This award is presented annually by the Small Business Administration to the small businessman in the state who has had more than routine success, and has made a recognizable contribution to the economy of the community.

northeast Pennsylvania and South Jersey. They also cover the northern portion of the state of Maryland and the state of Delaware; also parts of New York and West Virginia.

In 1946, at the age of 21, Herr bought a small potato chip business for $1,800. To make the purchase, he borrowed $1,700 from a friend, $200 from his father and used his savings of $200 for working capital. The annual sales of this small business at the time of purchase were approximately $1,500. The

As the company expanded, Jim Herr's reputation as an exceptional businessman grew as well. In 1969, he was named Pennsylvania's Small Businessman of the Year by the U.S. Small Business Administration.

Early packaging

Packaging, 2012

Tobacco Shed on the Herr Family Farm

First Plant in Nottingham, 1952

1956

1963

1963

*J.M. and Jim in front
of the new corporate office
in 1990*

1990

Plant #2 in Nottingham was opened in 2008.

Herr's Visitors' Center

Jim's favorite hobby allowed him to meet some famous golfers like Tom Watson.

Jim and Mim help Billy Graham celebrate his 90th birthday.

Early Chipper mascot at Phillies game

Jim and Mim have always been avid Phillies fans.

When Tommy Herr (a distant relative) played for the Phillies, he also helped advertise Herr's Chips.

Jim with President Gerald Ford

Jim with President Ronald Reagan

President George H. W. Bush greets Jim on Far East Trip

President Bush is the keynote speaker at
the 2000 Snack Food Convention in Philadelphia.

Jim and Mim with then Governor Bill Clinton

Jim and Mim with President George W. Bush and First Lady, Laura Bush

Air Force One

Jim with Governor Tom Ridge

*In 1994, Jim became a familiar face in TV advertising for Herr's.
Here he and Mim are taking a break from filming a commercial.*

candy. She would order all kinds of raw nuts, which my father would roast in a kettle of hot oil until he felt they were "just right." She would then cover these roasted nuts with chocolate and pack the candy in small white boxes labeled "Mrs. Herr's Chocolates." They were delicious, and our salesmen always had more orders than she could produce. That was the problem—she was the only one who made them and as she got older she could no longer keep up with it. Sometimes I think one of our family members should revive that line for us!

Expansion always involves a construction company, and I wanted to be able to count on one person to work with, rather than dealing with various subcontractors. That person was Paul Risk, a builder I met through my brother-in-law. He began working with me in the early 1960s, and his company continues to do work for us to this day (his son Steve now runs their company).

Paul was willing to take some time to get to know our industry, so he could understand our building needs. I asked him to visit some plants in New York and Canada, to see how they functioned. I also wanted him to get to know our key production employees, so they could work together on what we needed. I really didn't want to have to think all that through myself and I knew they would do a better job planning what we needed because they were involved with the details every day. The only request I made of Paul was that his company would not work for a competitor, and that didn't seem to ever be a problem for him.

When we had about a dozen trucks I talked with Paul about needing a building that would handle at least 25 trucks and a larger cooker.

At the time we were operating out of the 4,500-square-foot plant that had been expanded from our initial building in Nottingham. I also told him I thought we could grow 10 to 15 percent for the next 10 to 15 years. Paul did some figuring and then came back and asked if I really believed Herr's would experience such growth, because if I did we were talking about a much greater project. He said we would need to start in the middle of the property (just like my uncle had suggested years before!). I said, "But what will we do with the existing building? Shouldn't we use that?" Paul told me that if we really grew as projected, it wouldn't matter about the existing building. He was right; eventually it became a truck garage, then a maintenance shop, until it was razed to make space for our Visitors' Center.

In 1963 we quadrupled in size by building a 21,000-square-foot production facility in the middle of the property. In 1968 we added an additional 23,000 square feet for more cooking, packing, and potato storage space. A few years later we added 8,000 square feet of new stock rooms. I've always been grateful for Paul's close work with our engineers and production teams to build whatever we needed to accommodate our growth. Paul was a good listener and he worked well with our people.

In 1964, our sales really jumped when we embarked on a new packaging venture. For years we had sold chips in wax paper bags for 5, 10, and 15 cents a bag. We also offered a twin pack (two bags inside a larger cellophane package) for 49 cents. A packaging salesman convinced me that we should try selling chips in a 20-ounce cardboard barrel. The barrels resembled the popular wax-lined ice cream cartons and could be assembled affordably on site.

"King Style" barrels in production

The sturdy barrels would prevent chips from breaking and protect them from light (which causes them to become stale).

We called them "King Style" barrels and sold them for 99 cents. They became so popular, one of our salesmen told me that he was having trouble building a store display because customers pulled most of them from his cart as he was taking them from his truck into the store.

In 1966 our company hit a significant milestone when sales reached $1 million.

Ben Fenninger was the force behind our sales. He was so good at building routes that I asked him to train others and manage them. He trained some aggressive salesmen and routes expanded. One time Ben came to me and said we needed to expand into New Jersey. One of our good customers in Chester, Pennsylvania, wanted to open a store in New Jersey and wanted to sell our products.

I thought it was a little far out, but Ben convinced me we should do it. He had found a salesman who would drive from Nottingham to New Jersey, and he thought the area had a lot of potential. Sales grew there, and we rented a warehouse to store the chips, so the sales people could avoid the long drives. By 1968 we operated 35 sales routes out of Nottingham and five from New Jersey. Eventually we purchased a warehouse in Egg Harbor, New Jersey; it was our first branch and we operated 20 routes out of that location. We later built a larger warehouse in the same town to accommodate our growth.

Around the same time that we expanded to New Jersey, we began selling our products to the first Wawa convenience store. Over the years we have had the pleasure of growing with them and now serve over 500 of their stores.

The late 1960s marked the beginning of rapid territorial expansion that resulted in our opening new branch warehouses, purchasing trucks, and hiring people. In the 20 years after 1968, we grew from 35 routes to nearly 300, opened 12 new branches, and hired more than 500 people.

In the 20 years after that, 1988 to 2008, we added another 200 routes, opened eight additional branches, and hired another 500 people.

To support all this growth, we built a new plant in 1980 that allowed us to more than double our potato chip capacity and to create space for manufacturing other products as well.

Business Principles

Delegating is important to growth. Employees will make mistakes, but so will you! Remember that you are paying them for all the good things they are doing for the company. If they make a mistake now and then, forget it.

Always keep your word. If you can't make a payment on a loan, tell the person the reasons and make arrangements to repay it as soon as you can. Don't just ignore the problem. Make sure you pay your bills and treat people fairly.

Love forgives mistakes; nagging about them
parts the best of friends.

Proverbs 17:9

Herr children, 1961

Board of Directors, 1981

Chapter 8

DEVELOPING AS A FAMILY BUSINESS

You can tell from previous chapters that Mim and I have always operated as a team. As our family grew, she became less visible in the running of the company, but our home was always the source of my strength and support in business.

∽๐๑

A worthy wife is her husband's joy and crown; the other kind corrodes his strength and tears down everything he does.

Proverbs 12:4

∽๐๑

That naturally carried over into the way we raised our children. Early on, our children were exposed to the day-to-day decisions and issues we faced, just because they were at the same dinner table or in the same car as we discussed things. They also grew to know the employees, watched the buildings being built, avoided delivery vans when they rode their bikes, and smelled the chips cooking each day. There was very little separation between the Herr family and the Herr business.

I liked the idea of the family continuing to run the business, though I didn't want anyone to feel obligated to do so. Our oldest daughter,

June, went to college and became an English teacher and I don't think she ever thought seriously about working here full time. Our oldest son, J.M., said that he always thought he would be a part of the business and never considered doing anything else. After high school and two years of college, J.M. was unsure about continuing his education and I thought he would learn more by actually working in the business, so I encouraged him to become my apprentice instead of continuing. I know that J.M. regrets that he never finished college, but I guess I was influenced by my father's idea that experience was better than "book learning." Anyway, that's what we did, and it worked out OK for us, but J.M. and the rest of the second generation now have a program for the third generation entering management, requiring a bachelor's degree and at least two years of working successfully for another company before entering our management track.

When J.M. came on there were fewer than 100 employees and he knew everyone. He and I shared a small office and he learned a lot from listening, discussing issues, and observing people. Of course he had worked throughout his childhood by washing trucks, cleaning packing machines, and sweeping floors.

Gradually I turned some of the management over to J.M. One of his first responsibilities was overseeing our purchase of the Price & Englehart Company in Reading, Pennsylvania, manufacturers of a lard potato chip. The owners were a lot older than J.M. was, but he did a good job of working with them and trying to merge our two companies. We kept the Reading business going for some time, but eventually J.M. decided it was more cost effective to have this product made for us by another company.

J.M. began doing some hiring and worked with our advertising and purchasing departments. As people began reporting to him and I saw him growing in experience, I turned over the operations of the company to him, and then eventually he went from my assistant to Executive Vice President. In 1989 he became President, and in 2000, Chief Executive Officer.

Before J.M. came on board, I don't think we even had a budget. I certainly didn't know the words "strategic planning." That is not to say that we didn't have sound accounting and legal services from outside sources. Jack Ross, of Ross Buehler & Associates, has been invaluable to Herr's over the years; in fact, he is Mim's and my personal accountant to this day. Another professional, attorney Clarence Kegel, who began his career at a Lancaster law firm and later began his own firm, has offered legal advice to our company and our family for many years. In addition to their expertise in accounting and legal areas, part of Jack's and Clarence's effectiveness has been the result of their understanding and appreciation of our family culture.

But in addition to these outside specialists, J.M. saw the value of hiring an employee who could take our financial planning to a new level. He hired Gerry Kluis, who has now been our Chief Financial Officer for many years. We are very grateful for Gerry's guidance, not only in the financial area, but also as a senior leader in our company.

J.M. and I have always worked well together, perhaps because we have different management styles and we each respect what the other brings to Herr's. I am much more entrepreneurial and I tend

CEO & President

to make decisions more intuitively, whereas J.M. is better at planning and strategizing. We are both conservative in our business approach, being careful not to jeopardize the stability of our company. We want our employees to have a solid, healthy company to work for, so they don't have to worry that they're going to lose their jobs to a buy-out or a poor business decision.

Herr's has thrived under J.M.'s leadership. On our fiftieth anniversary in 1996, we employed 1,100 people and our annual sales had grown to $130 million. By the year 2000, sales increased to $150 million and, in addition to our geographic growth in the mid-Atlantic region, we grew in international markets such as Latin America.

Our middle son, Ed, became president in 2005, when J.M. became Chairman of the Board of Directors and I took the title of Founder. Ed had worked in the manufacturing area for a number of years, and then opened his own business for a while, before returning to the company to assist J.M. Among his many duties as President, Ed serves as our company spokesman, a role that I had enjoyed before handing it over to the next generation. Ed brings a fresh energy level to the management team, and he and J.M. are now close partners in running the business.

Our youngest son, Gene, has the responsibility of handling our most essential raw material—potatoes. People don't realize how important this job is to our whole operation, because if we're out of good quality potatoes, we're out of business! All the planning in the world can't alter that fact. I'm so glad that he has focused on that area of our company and provides that stability to the production process.

Gene Herr   *Daryl Thomas*

I have enjoyed more time to pursue personal interests such as charitable giving and travel, but I still love going to the office every day. I want to be available to Herr's as long as I am able to make a contribution, in whatever way people want me to.

Martha's husband, Daryl Thomas, started his career at the company operating a route truck before he served a few years in the Navy. When Daryl returned from the Navy, I asked him to start up and manage the Quality Assurance department, which served the company well and gave Daryl some great experience. He then moved into the marketing department and was eventually asked to head up Sales and Marketing. He was the first family member on the management team to earn a graduate degree, and he brings a lot of knowledge and good will to the position. He is a good mentor to several of our grandchildren and their spouses, who also are learning the business and getting their MBAs. It's encouraging to see the adventure continue through these young people! I think they will be good leaders in their time.

You might wonder what all this has to do with your career. Maybe you don't have the opportunity to develop a family business and you want to build an enterprise and then sell it when you retire. That's fine too, but I would just like to make the point that there is a tremendous advantage to running a business as a family. I've read that more than 90 percent of the companies in North America are family-owned, and that over two-thirds of all people starting businesses today grew up in a family business environment [*Encyclopedia of business.com. 2ed*]. That early exposure makes it easier for kids to learn the value of money management, of dealing with customers, of relations with employees, and just general knowledge of how to operate a business, such as working long hours.

Family businesses have a shared sense of traditions and values that often provide a stable foundation for decision-making. Also there's a strong commitment to making the business work, because your family cares about it, too. In addition, I think one of the biggest reasons we've decided to stay privately held is the control factor. We can make a decision to do something that reflects long-term thinking—something that may be expensive in the short term but will pay off later. This would not be possible if we had to answer to outside stockholders about our profits each quarter.

In 1981 I decided to expand the Board of Directors to include all five kids. One of the lawyers I mentioned this to said, "Go ahead and put 'em all on the board and watch 'em fight!" Well, I'm still watching, and so far there's been nothing but benefit to having all five on the board. June and Martha are not working in the business, but they

In 1996, the top management team consisted of: (Seated, left to right) J.M. Herr, President; Jim Herr, Chairman and CEO; Ed Herr, Vice President. (Standing, left to right) Richard White, Vice President - Sales and Marketing; Gerry Kluis, Vice President - Finance; and Harold Blank, Vice President - Manufacturing.

Jim Herr passed the Chairman's gavel to J.M. Herr as J.M. assumed the position of Chairman & CEO at the company's Board of Directors meeting on January 7, 2005. Directors, left to right: front row – John Stanton, Ed Herr, J.M. Herr, Jim Herr, Mim Herr, back row – June (Herr) Gunden, Bill Alexander, Jay Carr, Gene Herr, Martha (Herr) Thomas.

bring insights that we value and we feel that our business needs the interaction of all of its family members, not just those who work here every day.

∽o∾

Pride leads to arguments; be humble,
take advice and become wise.
Proverbs 13:10

∽o∾

Conventional wisdom says you should also have outside directors, and in 2001, we began adding folks to the Board who could give us direction from their expertise in business—some from higher education and some from other industries. They have been a great asset to us.

Going forward, I think our strength as a family is in our ability to work together and get along, despite differences. We now have 20 grandchildren and 18 great-grandchildren. I call Mim the "Queen," but she says her role is "Social Director" for the family, because she loves to plan get-togethers and family trips. The family bonds are crucial for the well-being of our family and of our business and we pray that they will stay strong.

Business Principles

Good relationships are a key to your success. The ability to get along with others, whether family or others, is vital.

If you have children who are interested in the business, give them the opportunity to learn and grow in the business. Be willing to turn your responsibility over to them, as they are able to handle it.

∽o∾

*The fool who provokes his family to anger and
resentment will finally have nothing worthwhile left.
He shall be the servant of a wiser man.*

Proverbs 11:29

Chapter 9

DECISION POINTS

∽o∾

Any enterprise is built by wise planning, becomes
strong through common sense, and profits
wonderfully by keeping abreast of the facts.

Proverbs 24:3, 4

∽o∾

I've already told you about some of the major decisions we had to make in our past—like rebuilding in Nottingham after the fire and choices about expanding. I'd like to elaborate on a few more decision points, because the success of any business depends on the incremental effect of day-to-day decisions.

In 1961 we decided to incorporate. There are many reasons why this is beneficial to a company, from tax benefits to liability issues. But for me, the whole impetus was so that we could start a profit-sharing plan for our employees. We needed the vehicle of shares of stock in order to best accomplish this.

With my farm background, I knew that farmers normally have a source for cash in their retirement years by capitalizing on their appreciated land values. I wanted to create something for our employees that would enable them to profit in their retirement from the increasing value of our company. The profit-sharing plan that we developed includes stock ownership of some of the company, so that as the stock rises in value, so do their assets. In addition to our profit sharing, which consists of company contributions only, we also have, as do most companies, a 401k plan. Between the two plans and Social Security, I believe our employees, especially those with a long tenure here, will have sufficient funds for retirement.

Usually, and fortunately, you have some time to ponder big decisions. One decision I had to make quickly involved whether or not to sell our products in the western Pennsylvania and eastern Ohio area. Around Christmas time in 1974 we got a call from a distributor who sold another brand of chips, saying that the other company was on strike and he couldn't get product. He had route salesmen who couldn't make a living if they didn't have chips to sell. Would we supply chips to them?

On the surface this looked like a golden opportunity, but we also wondered where it would lead in the long term. When the other company resolved its labor issues, where would this distributor's loyalty lie? We had to make a decision fast—they wanted product the next day— but clearly this had long-term implications. We decided to say yes, we'd help them out, but we sure didn't know how it was going to turn out. I put Curt Jones in charge of this project. A former Marine, at 6'4" Curt was imposing and could get right to the point, but he also worked well with people. He oversaw this uncharted venture into brand new sales territory, and with our first distributor of any size, at that. He did a great job and eventually we ended up with our own distribution facility in the Pittsburgh area. (Curt, after involvement in a number of other important projects, eventually left the company to become an entrepreneur/owner himself.)

On the heels of this decision, in 1976 someone called me and told me a company was for sale in Chillicothe, Ohio, about 50 miles south of Columbus. Because we have been able to grow without making acquisitions, and because that growth took capital, we never looked to purchase other companies. But J.M. and I went out to take a look at the facility and meet the owners. The company had been in business for quite a while, and was owned and operated by two brothers and one of their sons. They had their own brand and a clean, if not modern, facility. With our new distribution in the Ohio and western Pennsylvania area, we thought this made some sense.

We decided to purchase the company, and we knew who we wanted to run it. A man named John Thomas (son of our Mount Vernon friends) had started with us in route sales, then moved up to district manager, then branch manager, and we felt he could oversee both manufacturing and sales for this new operation. We changed their brand name to Herr's and that plant has been very helpful, especially now, as the Nottingham facility is often filled to capacity. John later moved back to Nottingham, served as our first Human Resources manager, and eventually retired after 42 years of service.

Many of our business decisions had to do with expenditures. Buying potatoes was always a determining factor in whether we made a profit, since potatoes are the raw material most basic to our company. I tried to become an expert on potatoes, learning the different varieties, how they grow, potato diseases, and where to purchase crops depending on the season of the year. Some potatoes are good for "table" use, but are not suitable for chipping.

When we were still in Willow Street, we met Bob Bare, an 18-year-old farm boy from Bird-in-Hand, Pennsylvania, when he and his younger brother, Jake, came to deliver a load of their farm's potatoes to us. At that time most farmers in Lancaster County grew a few acres of potatoes and Herr's would buy from the local farms when potatoes were in season. Bob suggested to his father, Elvin K. Bare, that they purchase a truck and become brokers for the local farmers. We developed a relationship and I saw that I could trust them to help keep us supplied with good potatoes.

When the Nottingham operation began we were using one and a half tractor trailer loads of potatoes a week. By the time of our major plant expansion in 1963, our needs had risen to several trailers a day, and I contracted with E. K. Bare & Sons to supply all our potatoes. They worked with us to develop growers in a number of states in the eastern U.S., and I was counting on them to keep our supply strong. After I made that deal with them, I began to worry about the consequences if something happened to the Bare brothers. What if there was an emergency? That's putting a lot of pressure on one source.

I leveled with Jake one day. I told him, "We're using an awful lot of potatoes, and what if something comes up that you can't supply them? Could we adjust our deal to allow others to supply some of

Unloading potatoes

them?" He graciously agreed, but they still supply the majority of our potatoes.

Currently we use up to 15 trailer loads of potatoes daily (over 75,000 tons annually). Our son Gene oversees the contracting for them, as well as the logistics, quality, and budgeting for this whole area of the business. He attends regional and national meetings with growers, fellow processors, and industry representatives from across the U.S. and Canada.

In addition to decisions about the potatoes, we have taken some bold steps in packaging. In 1974 we decided to change our bags from a glassine bag to a foil bag. Foil prevents light penetration, which is so important for keeping chips fresh over a long period. As you can imagine, one of our great challenges in chip sales is to keep the product fresh. Although the changeover was difficult and expensive and the additional cost for the foil was significant, we were convinced that it was important to consumers. Eventually packaging companies developed a metallized material that was cheaper than foil but had similar qualities for keeping the product fresh.

Only two years later we were faced with the difficult decision to discontinue the popular 99-cent barrel. The purchase price of the barrels had nearly quadrupled since ten years earlier, when we began using them. Reluctantly, we searched for a replacement. At first, we went to another type of round container, then a rectangular carton, and eventually discontinued that type of package altogether.

It was about the same time that we debated whether we should try to produce some of the products that were being made for us by other companies. We knew that we could make more money if we produced them ourselves, but should we venture into making other products? Could we sell enough to justify the cost of the equipment? What if the quality wasn't as good? We decided to try it and we began with cheese curls, followed by popcorn.

Foil Bag

In 1981 we decided to make pretzels, a process which requires a large baking oven rather than frying equipment. This was a major step for us and required a large learning curve for our production staff, but they were always eager to learn and try something new. In 1983 we began to manufacture corn products, such as corn and tortilla chips, and in 1984 we began making our own Onion Rings. Our latest venture was to make baked potato crisps, as well as extruded products made from corn or potato flour.

To make these latest new products, we were forced to face the biggest financial decision in our history: to build a whole new plant for the purpose of producing baked potato crisps as well as extruded snacks, like cheese curls. The plant was eventually completed in 2008 at a cost of nearly 20 million dollars, including equipment, but we delayed it several times due to a leveling off of sales, as well as cost pressures on raw materials. We finally decided to move ahead and we're glad we did—the plant is running nicely and growing in output every year. The plant was built in such a way that it can be easily expanded; hopefully we'll need to do that someday.

Our employees seem energized by new products—either ones we make or those we re-sell. It's fun for the sales force to have something new for their customers, and it keeps our production and marketing folks busy, creating new ways of handling products and new slogans and styles for packaging. In 1983 we changed our name from Herr's Potato Chips, Inc. to Herr Foods Inc., to reflect this commitment we have to our whole line of products.

When I think back over other decisions I've made, one comes to mind that occurred numerous times: whether or not to sell our company. Any company with a long history of growth will attract would-be buyers who like the idea of purchasing an established company. We often get calls from companies (or organizations working on behalf of a company) to see if we would be interested in selling the company.

For the longest time I'd tell them "No, my children are interested in running the business, and besides, I still enjoy what I'm doing." Now, as my children start to near retirement age, they are saying, "No, some of our third generation is interested, involved, and learning to run the company, and we're committed to keeping the business independent and family owned." Frankly, it takes a lot of work to keep a business independent. From a financial standpoint I would be better off to have sold it, but money and "things" are not as important to me as the continuation of a dream. Also, for our employees and our community, I believe we're better off being family and locally-owned. I know my children agree with that.

One of the business decisions that I'm proudest of came from a problem that gave me the most headaches. In 1983 waste disposal was a mounting concern for our growing company. The water from our production contains starch and other residue from the potatoes which makes it difficult to treat to the extent required for stream discharge. In addition to the waste water, we had potato peelings and other solid wastes to dispose of, such as product that doesn't pass quality control specs.

Through the years the company had purchased farmland in the vicinity of the plant, and we were using the waste water, from which most of the starch had been removed, to spray irrigate the land. I've always thought it would be neat to see cattle grazing on those fields, and I got to talking with one of our friends at church, Dennis Byrne, who is educated in the field of cattle, particularly Black Angus. I asked him if he thought Angus cattle would like to eat potato peelings and under-spec potato chips. Also, could they be fed crops grown on the farm if it was being irrigated with the waste water from the plant? Dennis began researching and worked with a nutritionist; they found an appropriate feed mix that would include not only corn and haylage grown on the farm, but our edible waste products.

Today Dennis Byrne runs the Herr Angus Farm, near the plant in Nottingham. Any product that we manufacture that does not meet quality standards is used to feed 500 head of cattle (the farm staff calls it "steer party mix"). Nearly one million gallons of water a week, which is used in our manufacturing process, is pumped to the farm to irrigate fields.

Because our business uses so many natural resources to produce and distribute our products, it's important that we stay sensitive to protecting our environment. It is very gratifying for Herr's to have found a solution to our waste products that contributes to the preservation and stewardship of our renewable natural resources. In addition to the Angus Farm, I'm also pleased that we found other ways to be careful with resources. For example, we reuse our corrugated shipping containers before selling them to be recycled. We use steam from our cooking process to heat water. And we've learned that the starch that is removed from the water in the potato processing area can be sold for fine paper manufacturing.

Herr Angus Farm

Sometimes when you think things are looking bleak, you can come up with a solution to a problem simply by talking with someone and exploring ideas together.

Business Principles

Solutions to business decisions take wisdom. If you reverence the Lord, He gives you ideas that you can't attribute to any other source.

The Lord helps you through the advice and insights of others He puts in your path.

∽∘∾

Get all the advice you can.
Proverbs 19:20

Chapter 10

SOME FLAVORFUL EXPERIENCES

In 1957 I listed a used 800-pound cooker for sale, and a man from Ohio bought it, with the purpose of taking it to Morocco, in North Africa, where he also had a home. When we finalized the sale, I told him to let me know if he ever had trouble with it—all he'd have to do is buy me an airline ticket to Morocco and I'd come help him. He said he knew all about machinery and certainly wouldn't have any trouble running this cooker.

Six months later he called and told me he had purchased a ticket for me to come to Morocco, that he needed help with the cooker. Never having been out of the country, I was enthused to go and I bought a ticket for Mim to go, too. We knew it would be a fascinating experience to travel in a culture so different from our own.

When we got there and looked at the cooker, it was squeaky clean, just like when we sold it to him. The man explained that he hadn't been able to use it, because whenever you try to start it, it jerks, and all the employees run out of the building expecting it to explode! I soon saw that there was a leak in the gas line, and when we fixed that the cooker worked like a charm.

We had a memorable trip to Africa, all because of that little gas leak. Another memorable experience took place in Latin America.

In the early 1960s I received a phone call from a business person I knew in Delaware. He told me that President John F. Kennedy was initiating a federal program called "Alliance for Progress," for the purpose of establishing economic cooperation between the United States and Latin (and South) America. Part of the program involved asking U.S. business owners to invest time and money in building businesses in other countries, to help that country's economy and to forge an alliance with our country. Specifically, the caller asked, would I be willing to partner with a Panamanian to start a potato chip operation in Panama City? There were five Delaware partners who said they would contribute money, if I would just provide the expertise.

Mim and I thought about this for a while and decided we liked the idea, because of the adventure it offered and also the thought that we could help our country—even if it was a small contribution. We traveled to Panama and met our Latin partner, whose wife and children graciously invited us into their home. He was excited about the opportunity ahead, and I made plans to send our plant engineer, Charlie Temple, to help put together the plant and equipment.

It wasn't long before the cost of the venture increased beyond the expectations of the Delaware partners, and they got cold feet and backed out. I decided to continue and became co-owner with our Panamanian partner. Over the next few years, Mim and I made quite a few trips there, even taking our two youngest children with us to live in Panama City for a short time.

At one point when the operation was going pretty well, I saw that they had extra capacity in the plant that wasn't being used and they needed to generate more sales. I agreed to provide some additional funding so that the business could purchase another truck, to be used to develop sales. The next time I arrived in Panama I asked about the truck, and it turned out the money was used to purchase a boat. Our partner was convinced he could get more customers by taking them fishing! I told him we couldn't *afford* to take anyone fishing— we needed a truck to deliver product to the stores. This was one of several cultural differences that we didn't know how to handle.

A major problem vexing the Panama operation was the length of time it was taking to get potatoes to the plant. We started out buying potatoes from the same broker we used in the States and made a deal with the container shipping company to keep the potatoes cool during transit. If they weren't kept cool, the potatoes would rot and run out of the container like water.

The shipping agreement didn't solve the problem. Sending potatoes by boat from Florida just took too long. If potatoes aren't used within a day or two of taking

Panama potato warehouse in Boquete

them out of the ground they must be stored properly or they will turn brown, making a very off-color product.

Realizing we would need a local source for potatoes, we were put in touch with another Panamanian, who had a degree in agriculture and knew a lot about the soil and farming conditions locally; he also spoke English very well. We felt confident he could help us, and we partnered with him to buy a 200-acre farm in the fertile, mountainous region of Boquete, about an 8-hour drive north of Panama City. Our new partner was excited to be able to grow a crop for which he had a ready market, and we trusted his ability to get us good potatoes for the plant. And the colorful, endearing locals were somewhat curious to see what we Americans were doing there. They watched as our partner engineered an irrigation system from the top of the mountain to the potato growing areas, and the indigenous Indians who lived in the steep parts of the mountains would shyly come to apply for work in the fields. The women, with their colorful handmade dresses, would silently watch from the shelter of coffee trees nearby. We so enjoyed the pristine beauty of that place. At one time we took our five children and their spouses on a unique vacation there.

I soon learned that my partner was very full of ideas, not only for growing potatoes, but for any other business venture that captured his attention. He was very gregarious and well-known, and at one point, with his contacts in government, he thought he could control the entire vegetable market for the country. As he got more involved in these bigger deals, he lost interest in the potato growing business. I could see that he was thinking too big and had too many irons in the fire.

One day I learned that the farm had been sold, without anyone letting me know! I never received any money. I asked how the farm could be sold without my consent, since I was co-owner, and I was told that my signing off on the sale wasn't needed in Panama, that I would probably get paid someday. Needless to say, I'm not holding my breath.

I'm not sure what they did with the chip plant. It was functioning for a while, but I know it was a headache for them, so I don't know if they kept it very long. Eventually, I learned that my farming partner got into the bed-and-breakfast business.

We lost money on the Panama venture, but I wouldn't trade the experience for anything! I'm not sorry we did the project, but it did make me realize that culture plays a big part in the way we do business. It gives me great respect for successful international companies.

Another experience that lost money, but was "flavorful" for our family, took place right in Nottingham. It started when I saw an ad in the newspaper for a herd of ponies. The cost was $7,000 for ten mares and two stallions, which was expensive, but I thought we could breed them and make some money. I also enjoyed the thought of presenting them to the kids, because we already had one pony, Jenny, at the time, and the kids loved her, but she was getting old. One Saturday I told the kids that I had twelve surprises for them coming that day. It was so much fun to see their excitement when ponies started arriving!

True to my plan, our ponies multiplied and we had as many as forty at one time. But, not according to my plan, many other people were raising ponies as well, and the prices dropped to almost nothing. The children outgrew the ponies and we almost gave the ponies away to get rid of them. We even used them as prizes for some contests at Herr's. We hired a promotional firm to help devise a win-a-pony contest that we put on the back of chip bags.

I guess if there is a silver lining to that cloud it is that two of our children, J.M. and Martha, have a life-long love of horses as a result of this experience. In fact, Martha has built a career on this passion of hers: she and a partner are brokers who buy show horses in Europe for American clients. They also run a training program on the horse farm that Daryl and Martha own.

Business Principles

Every company has a "culture." Identifying your values and staying true to them helps give your company a firm footing.

Not all your ideas will work out, no matter how well-intentioned you are!

Shown here, the former Mira-Pak offices and manufacturing facility.
Herr plans to sell the building, keep the operation small in the early stages of growth.

James S. Herr

On October 15, 1980, James S. Herr, President of Herr's Potato Chips, announced that he had purchased the assets of the Houston firm with the expressed intention of returning it to its former prominence.

The first step has already been taken. Mira-Pak's first new packaging machine will roll off the line in April. But Herr admits that the rebuilding will be slow.

"We've started with about 23 people (compared with 200 previously)," explains Herr, "many of them former Mira-Pak employees. For now, we're looking to assemble a team of well-qualified people to put Mira-Pak back to its original status in the industry.

Report on Mira-Pak purchase from a trade journal, 1980.

Chapter 11

MISTAKES ARE PART OF IT

Sometimes I think people get the impression that if you have a successful company, you must have done everything right. Well that certainly isn't true of me, as you know from the Panama venture and my idea to raise ponies. I think mistakes are just part of life, especially if you tend to take risks. The key is what you do after you've made a mistake. My father-in-law, a man of succinct speech, gave me some wise advice about that: "In a bad situation, just make a deal and settle."

If we learn from our mistakes, they aren't totally wasted. I'll tell you about a few of mine.

The first was with a packaging company. One of the major suppliers of packaging equipment in our industry (and for our company) was Mira-Pak, a company based in Houston, Texas. In 1980 it went into bankruptcy and the common reasoning for it was that they had simply not made the changes necessary to compete with other companies in the industry. However, they still had some good people, and several of the members of Mira-Pak's sales force approached me about buying the company, saying that it would be a blessing to the whole industry if I would purchase it. We would run the business with the current employees.

I was somewhat intrigued by the idea and went to the court's bankruptcy auction and took along my banker. We learned that it would take a million dollars to buy the company. My banker was a free spirit. Having just returned from vacation, he hadn't checked in with his bank superiors, but he said loaning me a million dollars wouldn't be a problem. He also suggested that I buy a condo in Houston for about $30,000, so I'd have a place to stay when I went to Houston. I thought it was interesting that a banker was trying to spend more of my money, but it did make some sense since it was close to the Mira-Pak company.

The purchase of the company included two buildings—one big, nice building and a smaller one—and I didn't feel we needed both. To raise capital, I sold the larger structure to a company who made motors for drilling companies (they put electronic components on gas and oil drilling rigs). The drilling industry in Houston had been booming prior to this, but the bottom fell out shortly after they purchased the building. The people I had sold it to called and told me they had to back out of the deal and they were going to file for bankruptcy. I took the building back and eventually sold it to the city of Houston.

I still had the Mira-Pak business in the second building, and for a while it looked like we were going to make it. But then some of the engineers decided to quit the company, and they had been a big factor in my decision to buy it.

To add to the Mira-Pak debacle, the production people at Herr's began telling me that even *they* didn't want to keep buying Mira-Pak equipment. They had learned of a better weighing process offered by a Mira-Pak competitor and they felt it was in Herr's best interest to change vendors.

Finally, I just had to admit it was time to pull the plug on the effort to save Mira-Pak. I eventually sold the buildings, our condo, and chalked the whole thing up to a learning experience. The lesson? Probably that we should have done better due diligence and evaluated the situation less emotionally. I am by nature quite inquisitive and there are many different things I'd like to try. When I see a business opportunity, it's very tempting for me to jump in with both feet and not spend a lot of time thinking about it.

Secondly, I have made some mistakes in the oil and gas well industry, which I've been involved with for more than three decades.

During the 1970s, the man who ran the advertising agency our company was using invited J.M. and me to dinner at a fancy Philadelphia restaurant to introduce us to a friend of his. He thought we'd be interested in his friend because he was a Christian and was very philanthropic.

There were about ten people at the dinner. The man we were all being introduced to was a smooth-talking, charismatic Texan, who promptly told us he didn't believe in banks but he believed in helping his Christian brothers make money. That comment alone should have made us question whether what he was about to suggest was a good idea. But he knew his Bible inside and out and talked a lot about religious themes, which I guess dispelled some of our reservations.

He told us he wanted to help people invest in the oil and gas business. He had a connection with a well-known Texas family, who made a lot of money in the oil business, and it was his aim to use his connections "to help God's little people." We were impressed enough that we went to Texas to see him, and I remember he had a Lincoln with no license plates—he said he didn't believe he needed them, that he had a right to drive. That should have been another red flag.

Still, he sounded as if he knew what he was doing, and both J.M. and I believed him. Well, he knew what he was doing all right: he was getting us to invest in his oil wells, and we ended up losing most of that money. The sad part was that he had also convinced a number of missionaries with little money to invest in his company, telling them that he wanted to provide an income for them. They lost their investments.

This guy was also involved in wells in West Virginia, and when his business failed, I received some equity in the West Virginia gas wells. I decided to join several other people to start a company, the Interstate Drilling Company; we thought that at least we could recoup the money for the missionaries. Eventually I took control of the company and became chairman of the board and saw to it that those debts were repaid.

I remained involved in the Interstate Drilling Company until 2001 when I sold my share of the company.

And finally I'll tell you about a costly mistake from trusting someone who turned out to be involved in a Ponzi scheme. In the 1980s I learned of an organization that helped non-profits with fundraising and also advised corporations about charitable organizations they considered especially worthy of funding. The man who ran this organization came very well recommended by some influential people, and I'm always interested in how to best handle our charitable giving.

The head of this organization told me that he knew quite a few people who were very wealthy and very philanthropic, but who just didn't have the time or inclination to do a lot of research into which organizations they wanted to contribute to. So they told this "facilitator" that if he found people who were also contributing large sums of money to good causes, they would match, or essentially double, that contribution.

I would need to deposit my money with the organization for six months, proving to the other contributors that the money was available for gifting, and allowing the organization to match up donors. Then the donor would make their contribution and the organization would send the doubled amount to whatever charity I wanted to fund. The story sounded somewhat plausible to me, because I know that charitable giving, if you are conscientious about it, does take a lot of time and effort.

It was exciting to me, of course, to have my charitable giving doubled! The more I saw this happen, the more money I wanted to give through the organization. I also knew others in the Philadelphia area who were experiencing the same benefits, and momentum seemed to be building. The organization boasted that it was giving away more money than the Carnegies, Mellons, and Rockefellers.

We didn't know that the facilitator had begun siphoning off funds for his personal use, which eventually totaled millions of dollars. We did know that the time period of the initial deposit had gone from six months to nine and ten months; later we learned that he had begun using current deposits to pay off earlier charitable contributions, instead of sending the money to the intended charity.

Eventually the house of cards fell and our facilitator went to jail. The judge ordered that those of us whose target charities received the doubled money had to pay some of it back to those whose charities had not received any of the benefits they were promised. Several of us went further and made a commitment to pay back everything that was lost to those charities whose donors we personally had introduced to this organization.

Looking back, it's easy to see that this really was "too good to be true" and as the saying goes "when it looks that way, it probably is." It was a hard lesson to learn.

Business Principles

If you make a mistake, admit it, learn from it, and move on.

Be careful about entering into a new venture; do your homework and don't invest more than you can afford to lose.

A man who refuses to admit his mistakes can never be successful.
But if he confesses and forsakes them, he gets another chance.

Proverbs 28:13

Jim with Franklin Graham of Samaritan's Purse

Chapter 12

MONEY!

∽◦∽

Trust in your money and down you go!
Trust in God and flourish as a tree!

Proverbs 11:28

∽◦∽

I didn't tell you that when I was 15 and I read that verse from Psalm 37 about "the desires of your heart," I had a pretty elevated desire in my heart. I told the Lord that I would like to earn a million dollars and that I would like to give a million dollars away. I guess I was tired of being poor.

Money has motivated me, there's no doubt about it. Companies need to be profitable to thrive, and I want our employees (including me) to earn a good living. I enjoy the challenge of taking a struggling entity and making it profitable. The goal of being profitable is what keeps our company disciplined and focused.

I think that the reason the word "profit" has become a bad word in some circles today is that the desire for money can easily take precedence over higher goals. Money, instead of being a tool, can become an end in itself, a slave driver that takes away your good judgment and moral values. It can rob you of your joy. It can truly become your master, rather than your servant.

Mim has a few quotes from people on our refrigerator door, and for years she has had this one there: "The only way to avoid the tyranny of money is to ruthlessly give it away" (Vernon Broyles, pastor at North Avenue Presbyterian Church, Atlanta, Georgia). I think it's good to remind ourselves that money can become a tyrant, and it is a ruthless one that destroys people. Instead we need to be "ruthless" (in the sense of being unrelenting) in giving it away.

You might think, "That's something I'll worry about when I have more of it," but I would like to encourage you to give some of your money away even when you are earning very little. This was a principle that our church taught us early on, that tithing (giving a tenth of your income to the Lord) was a discipline a Christian should practice. So Mim and I were careful to do this, even when we were still living on my brother's farm. We learned over the years that there is great joy in giving money away, regardless of the amount you give.

∽o∾

Honor the Lord by giving him
the first part of all your income.
Proverbs 3:9

∽o∾

About twenty years ago I formed the James S. Herr Foundation as a vehicle for more intentional giving. While the foundation serves primarily as a charitable organization that supports the interests of Mim and me, occasionally there is some overlap between the foundation and the company. (The company has its own charitable giving program, which disperses support to hundreds of local organizations.)

Funding for the James S. Herr Foundation comes primarily from my own funds and our focus over the years has been to spread the good news that Jesus is the Master of the Universe and that He cares about each person in His creation. He cares so much that He died to provide for each person a way to be forgiven and to become part of His family. In my opinion, there is no better way to use money than to get this message out, and there is no better way to live than to become involved in His cause.

Years ago Mim and I were introduced to the ministry of Stephen Olford, a dynamic preacher who we felt was doing a great job of getting the gospel message out. We wanted to support this work, and I have enjoyed many years of serving on the Board of Directors for the Stephen Olford Center for Biblical Preaching in Memphis, Tennessee.

Some of the other ministries that have meant the most to us are Sandy Cove (a Christian camping ministry in North East, Maryland), Lancaster Bible College, the John Edmund Haggai Institute for Advanced Leadership Training in Atlanta, Georgia, and Samaritan's Purse, in Boone, North Carolina.

More than 50 years ago I was influenced by a group of Mennonite business people who had a heart for using their business skills to help others around the world. One such person was Erie Sauder, who started Sauder Woodworking Company, in Archbold, Ohio. He was a founder of an organization called MEDA, Mennonite Economic Development Association. His passion was to develop the wasteland of Chaco, Paraguay, into habitable and profitable land. Sauder made 18 visits to Chaco, working with the native Paraguayan Indians to develop their colonies. Other founders of MEDA were Sanford High, who started the High Welding Company, Orie Miller, who ran a shoe factory, and Ivan Martin, who had a limestone business. They were service-oriented Mennonite business people who wanted to use their business skills to create solutions to poverty.

I've been particularly interested in Africa, and have taken five trips there for MEDA causes. Once we went to Somalia to help a man who wanted to start a hammer mill in his little hamlet. I remember eating on a plate in his hut that was made of cow dung, and really it was OK! It was so invigorating to me to see someone get a start who could then develop a small business to help others make a living. I'm still involved in MEDA, though I don't travel as much anymore.

There are so many other good organizations and causes that it can take all your time just trying to absorb the information about them. I thoroughly enjoy this season of my life, when I can use the resources we've been given and figure out ways to be a blessing with them.

I have said many times that you can never outgive the Lord. He always gives back more, not only in more earnings, but in a richer quality of life. You don't have to be a millionaire to know this. Perhaps you have already found that when you give your time or money or efforts to help others, you get back so much more.

∽○∾

It is possible to give away and become richer!
It is also possible to hold on too tightly and lose everything.
Yes, the liberal man shall be rich!
By watering others, he waters himself.
Proverbs 11:24, 25

∽○∾

I have enjoyed serving on boards of various ministries and community organizations, because it's a way I can contribute, in addition to giving money. I also think it's healthy for a company to be involved in the life of their community. As a company, you are a citizen and there may be ways you can help your local neighbors to enjoy a better quality of life.

Jim presents a check to Larry Spaid, of the local hospital

One of Herr's projects that we enjoy most is that we light up the trees on our campus for Christmas so that people can drive through with their families (without charge) and be blessed during that special season of the year. Our granddaughter's husband is in charge of it, and Mim, who loves Christmas anyway, gets excited every year when they start putting up the lights.

We also team with Chester County at July 4 to put on a "Freedom Fest" at Nottingham Park. We bring in music and we have fireworks and food and over 10,000 people attend. It's something we can enjoy with our community while we also celebrate and honor our great country.

In addition to giving to the community, we always want to be sure to treat our employees fairly. We attempt to adjust wages with the cost of living increases, but, much as you would like to, you have to be careful not to promise too much. Unexpected increases in the cost of goods and other factors can diminish cash reserves and undermine the health of the company. The best gift you can give your employees is to keep the company good and solid, so they don't have to worry about their job security. It's gratifying that in 65 years, we have had no lay-offs due to a lack of business.

In recent years management has instituted more programs for Herr's employees. Dick White, a long-term senior management member who is now Vice President of Human Resources, has been diligent about making the best programs available to our employees. A *Helping Hands* program aids employees with unplanned emergencies or financial setbacks. A *Partners in Service* program pays those who want to donate time to charitable organizations. A ministry staff is available to provide confidential religious counseling for those who ask. Also, scholarships are given to children of employees. This is all in addition to a very competitive fringe benefit program.

I've seen business owners who take a lot of money out of their businesses, even from the start, but our philosophy has been to be conservative and plow as much as we can back into the company. That way we're prepared if we need to expand or if we need a new piece of equipment.

Although we have taken on debt over the years to purchase new equipment and buildings, I have tried to be prudent about it and not allow the company to become too leveraged. More than once banks have encouraged us to take on more debt because we had a strong balance sheet (after all, that's what they're in business to do), but you have to be careful not to get overextended.

∽o∾

The wise man saves for the future,
but the foolish man spends whatever he gets.
Proverbs 21:20

∽o∾

There is a proverb that says "He who gathers money little by little makes it grow" (Proverbs 13:11, NIV). I think one of the pitfalls people fall into is that they try to get too big too quick. I like the idea of "plugging away" at something, not trying to make an impression or get rich quick, but being more methodical and careful about growth.

Steady plodding brings prosperity;
hasty speculation brings poverty.

Proverbs 21:5

∽o∼

There are times when this doesn't feel exciting or glamorous, but that has to be OK. I remember times over the years when I wondered "What in the world am I doing making potato chips?" There were other people doing things I thought were a whole lot more significant or impressive. But we just went to work every day, regardless of those occasional thoughts. I don't think anyone feels positive all the time, and you have to just go on and do what you know you need to do. I also felt a lot of responsibility for those whose livelihood now depended on Herr's. It wasn't just about me—it was about all of us together.

I mentioned earlier that in my teens I enjoyed playing in Mr. Simmons' orchestra, and here is a song we used to sing (I still sing it to myself):

There are many things I'd like to do
As my journey I pursue.
I would like to be a leader
As any normal man would do.
I would like to be a millionaire
With a million to bestow.
But I'd rather be an old-time Christian, Lord,
Than anything I know.

Business Principles

Be careful with your money. Don't let it master you.
Don't spend it all. Keep your business good and strong by
having a solid financial foundation.

Give to others, both as a company and as an individual. Learn
the joy that comes from being generous.

Avoid the temptation to try to get "big" quickly. Just concern
yourself with doing the best you can with what you're given to
do *today*, and your company's size will take care of itself.

Jim and Mim with 2nd generation family members in the busine Left to right: J.M. Her Gene Herr, Ed Herr an Daryl Thomas (marri to Martha)

Chapter 13

LOOKING AHEAD

People ask me what I see when I look forward—for myself, our family, our company, and our industry. Also, what message would I offer you, as you look ahead in your own life?

For myself and my family, I just want us to always keep moving forward in this adventure of living for the Lord. Even though there are days, at age 87, when I have health issues, I want to always be energized by the things that matter in life: the value of making a difference in someone else's life, either by giving financially or by helping in the myriad of other ways we can serve. Business and service should never be separated.

As for Herr's and for the industry, I know that we are operating in a very competitive environment these days. While consolidation in the snack food industry has resulted in many fewer companies than when I first began, it doesn't mean that it is less competitive. The companies that have survived and thrived have done so because they're good at what they do. In addition to the traditional snack food companies, other large food companies have also entered the market with various snack-like products. The truth is the market overall is more competitive than it's ever been.

The future of Herr's will depend on our leadership, on the work ethic of our employees, on the political climate of our country, and on our use of resources. It will depend on our ability to weather the storms that will inevitably come and our willingness to look for opportunities that will also come.

As I envision the future, I see the need to continue our growth through expansion of our sales territories and product innovations. We will need to pay constant attention to details in every department of our business and always be willing to learn. We need to do everything in our power to keep our country from over-regulating business and therefore destroying personal initiative. Hard work and high goals have never been more important.

People are our most valuable asset and we must continue to encourage and empower our employees. Several years ago Don Cartusciello, who was new to our company at the time, asked me to jot down what I consider to be "Laws of Good Business." As you can see on the following page, my main concerns are that we treat our employees and our customers well and that we manage our finances properly.

∞∞

Watch your business interests closely.
Know the state of your flocks and your herds.
Proverbs 27:23

1 Follow the Golden Rule.
Treat others the Way you would
like to be treated.

2. Start out with Integrety

3. Have a good business model

4. Be Honest and always pay
your bills on time.

5. Have good financial Controls.

6. Earn the respect of your lenders
or financial institution.

7. As you grow try to have the
employees involved so they are a
part of the team.

8. Make sure employee's have good
working Conditions

9. If everyone works hard to achieve
the quality products you desire
Share profits with them some way.

10. We are all in this together.

11. Try to assess our Customers
needs and make sure they are
Pleased with the product at the end
of the day.

12. Hope everyone is Happy.
And can smile.

Jim Herr's "Laws of Good Business," 2009

I think the best chance of long-term success for Herr's is for us to remain an independent, family-owned business. At this time we already have ten of the third generation active in the business, including both descendants and spouses, and I wouldn't be surprised if that number grows. That is very encouraging to me, and I have high aspirations for our business and our family. I pray that they will continue our values and culture.

Most of my values have come from my faith, and it would be dishonest to take personal credit for them. All I can tell you is that I have seen how Biblical truths have played out in my life, and that it is God who directed my paths. Financial success is a very small part of being successful. The most satisfying way to live is to know you're in a relationship with the Creator and that you are pleasing God. Delight yourself in Him by reading His book and by seeking His wisdom. See what desires He plants in your heart and how He goes about giving those to you. Learn to see life as an adventure!

Starting a business may not be what God wants you to do—it just happens to be what He called me to do. Your gifts may be in creating a wonderful home environment for your family, or using an innovative idea as you teach school, or beginning a ministry of some kind. Perhaps you are working for a company and you can make a difference by being open to new ideas for doing your job better. I encourage you to use the creativity you were born with to find your passion and work hard at it.

I see this in our own family. While our three sons are active in our snack food business, our two daughters have chosen very different career paths. Both have started a business in the area in which they are gifted: one in the equestrian field and one in editorial services. Also, in our third generation (our grandchildren) I am delighted to see many varied interests, in fields like ministry, drama, education, finance, nursing, homemaking, dietetics, marketing, and engineering. In addition two couples of the third generation have started their own businesses.

We have stressed all along that while family members are welcome to join the business, what we truly desire is that they'll be happy doing whatever they choose to do. For those who do choose to join the company, we have written rules that govern all aspects of getting and keeping a job, requirements for moving up to take on more responsibility, and so on. We have a "family constitution" and a Family Council made up of our second generation siblings. The key to success in this area is good communication, fairness, and transparency. Mim and I are so pleased, not just with those who have joined the company, but also with those who haven't.

I'll leave you with my definition of success: Success is finding out what God wants you to do, and then doing it. Simple, but it takes a lifetime of work!

God bless you!

Business Principles

If you have a family business, be careful not to assume that everyone in the family will want to make it their career. After all, I didn't continue working on my father's farm, but I pursued something I personally wanted to do.

Never stop looking for opportunities to be a blessing to someone else!

Epilogue

(I asked Mim to write this epilogue, since many folks who know us best think she is our "better half"!)

MIM'S NOTES

What's it like to have been married to Jim Herr for 64 years? It's been a career of its own, in a sense. It never occurred to me to pursue anything other than being an encourager and supporter to my husband and our children. That's what my mother, his mother, and all my aunties did.

Our five children were born before the advent of epidurals, but I *was* in a hospital, which is more than my mother could say. When I was five years old, my mother gave birth to identical twin girls (so identical she tied a pink ribbon around the wrist of one of them). My older sister and I were helpful (that's the way we remember it) in changing diapers, feeding them, and rocking them to soothe them. I chose to respond primarily to the younger twin. Two years later Mother gave birth to identical twin boys. This time I was responsible for cuddling and caring for the older one. So I did have experience in taking care of infants by the time our own children came along.

My heart never ceases to praise God for answering our on-the-knees prayers for safe deliveries of healthy babies—five wonderful, varied, lovable children, who continue to bring us much joy. I tried to use Proverbs 14:1 as a guide: "A wise woman builds her house, while a foolish woman tears hers down by her own efforts." I repeat "I tried," but not all of my judgments and priorities were as good as I wish they were. I tell the children that what I didn't do right they could use as a learning experience—lame logic, huh?

Our household was always in a state of "managed bedlam" while the kids were young. The big mongrel house dog shed hairs, the little pink Easter chicks had free roaming, the kittens were born in the house, an effort was made to hatch duck eggs in a warmer on the kitchen counter—and then there was Tojo, the monkey. His cage rested on the table between the recliners in the TV room. He'd put his little claw through the cage and hold Jim's finger while they watched the evening news together. Our enjoyment of him waned over the months, especially after he escaped from the cage and raced around the house. Since it was summer we thought he would enjoy living in the trees outdoors and hopefully make his way south by winter. NO, he *liked* us and sat on the door knob looking in, or snatched a half sandwich from our picnic table, or landed out of nowhere on an unsuspecting visitor's shoulder. We finally resorted to paying the SPCA to find a home for him. Our German shepherd pup never did learn to obey. His name was Prince, but he didn't act very princely when he threatened to bite our guests. The Shetland ponies we had didn't involve me, thankfully.

At my present age, I can't believe I put up with such a menagerie in addition to five children—not to mention gardening, canning, freezing, and doing bookwork. But I had energy then.

Meals were predictably regular and around the kitchen table. Sometimes Jim would call in the afternoon and ask what was for supper—could he bring Urb Anzmann (a packaging rep) or another business associate to the house with him? I can only imagine some of their thoughts as we just put out one more place at our simple kitchen table. But they kept coming back, and the kids and I learned to know many of Herr's business associates this way.

At evening meals our practice was to read a Bible story from *Egermier's Story Book* (given to us by Jim's mother) and have a prayer. Then quite often Jim left for a meeting—school board, church committee, etc. There was usually quite a lot of household activity when he hurried off, but by the time he got home the kids' schoolwork was done and the cafeteria change was laid out for the next day. Toys were put away, the kitchen was clean, and all five were in bed. It was then that we had a chance to converse without interruption.

In later years, Jim sometimes questioned whether all his church and community involvements (in addition to his time at the business) were detrimental to the kids, since he did not have long hours in the evenings to be home with them. It's a question with no definitive answer, but I don't remember ever sensing that the children felt resentful or deprived because he was at a meeting. I know they were proud of their father; in fact, there's a proverb that says, "A child's glory is his father" (Proverbs 17:6). I'm sure they could sense that I was positive about what he was doing, and I think a mother's attitude is often "caught" by the children.

I also don't remember ever resenting that I was so "occupied" at home, while Jim was on the move. He felt a responsibility to be involved in local community work (later branching out into national and international involvements), and I was contented in my role. He encouraged me and expressed appreciation often. Besides, I wasn't as gregarious and outgoing and self-confident as he was. He is the one who has brought me out of my timidity and helped me find that I did enjoy stepping outside the role of homemaker (though "homemaker" is still my favorite classification).

Anyone reading this who is from a large family, even a family wholly dedicated to God, knows that everything is not always peaches and cream. A large family means a lot of doors opening and closing, some quarreling between siblings, teenagers sometimes choosing a temporary detour from what they were taught, illnesses, and disappointments. And I lost patience, chose improper discipline, disagreed with Jim on financial indebtedness (I was always leery of *any* indebtedness)—I certainly wasn't perfect! However, the strange but happy truth is that now I have to deliberately *try* to recall unpleasant memories (because I was told that I have to be realistic in this book). When I think back, honestly all that I remember is good.

When our youngest started school I began volunteering for the Red Cross. At the time we were called "Gray Ladies," for the color of our uniforms. I volunteered once a week at the local hospital in West Grove. Toward the end of the 20+ years I limited my time to helping at Bloodmobiles. (I even donated a couple gallons of blood during that time.)

Another outside-the-home activity was attending Lancaster Bible College. Upon applying I learned that in order to attend daytime credit courses I needed a high school diploma—duh! So I first tested out and got a GED diploma. It was a one hour drive one way to the college each day. I only took three courses, but I really enjoyed them even though I was old enough to be the mother of the rest of the students.

I began giving addresses at banquets, church services, or community clubs, but mostly at women's meetings. I have no idea how it came about that I could make an inspirational speech that would bless others. I found I was pretty good at memorizing and inserted poetry and stories into the speeches (maybe because my father gave us pop quizzes on math or Bible verses during meal time all through my childhood). In any event, I spent quite a bit of time preparing for speeches and accepted invitations for many years—until I felt I was too old to be gallivanting around the country, especially for night meetings. At the same time, Jim was invited to speak at business functions; I guess we were on a roll.

When our firstborn was six months old, Jim wanted me to go with him to a Potato Chip Institute convention in Cleveland, Ohio. (This would be the first of many conventions and the beginning of his many involvements with the organization.) Now I had never been more than a two- or three-hour drive from my home until our honeymoon! So to think of leaving the baby with a grandmother and go to a *convention* was a big decision. Obviously I survived and learned to relax and be comfortable in crowds. Throughout the years we were blessed with the availability of trustworthy people who would move in and take over the care of our household. Our travels took us pretty much around the world. Quite often the travel was for Jim's work within the snack food industry, his interest in economic development connected to the church, and his role with the National Federation of Independent Business. Our participation in the Alliance for Progress program took us to Panama repeatedly for several years.

When our "favorite five" were between the ages of 8 and 18 we began family trips, the first being an extended motor home trip across the U.S. Then there began the weddings and grandchildren, and we developed planned family vacations once a year. These were most often in the States (particular memories stand out of dude ranches in Idaho and Wyoming, as well as a cruise in Alaska), but we did go to Israel for a Holy Land tour, to a favorite resort in Acapulco, to South Africa on safari, and to Scotland for a golf holiday. A couple of missions-oriented trips were to the Dominican Republic with Hope International and to Maui, Hawaii, with the Haggai Institute. By God's good graces we enjoyed health and safety in all our travels. The trips abroad were ever so exciting, but possibly the most relaxing and simplest vacations are the times we've spent at the Greenbrier Resort in West Virginia. In the summer of 2011 fifty-seven of our then fifty-nine family members were able to join us there. (Since then our number has grown to sixty-one, and we've learned of another one on the way.) Jim and

I say that one of our happiest times in our advanced years is to "sit back" and watch the family interacting in such a happy way.

We live in the same house we started in when we came to Nottingham. It's old, but it's *familiar*. We can still host the family for outdoor picnics (with the help of everyone), but we *have* outgrown room for seating at dinners and I have started this last year to use a caterer and the tour center next door for dinners. Family gatherings are the moments I cherish!

At age 85, I am thankful for the richness of life, the *flavor*, if you will. Jim and I pray that your life will be just as rich, just as seasoned with the blessings that will come as you follow your own personal calling.

APPENDIX

Family Tree of
James S. & Miriam Herr

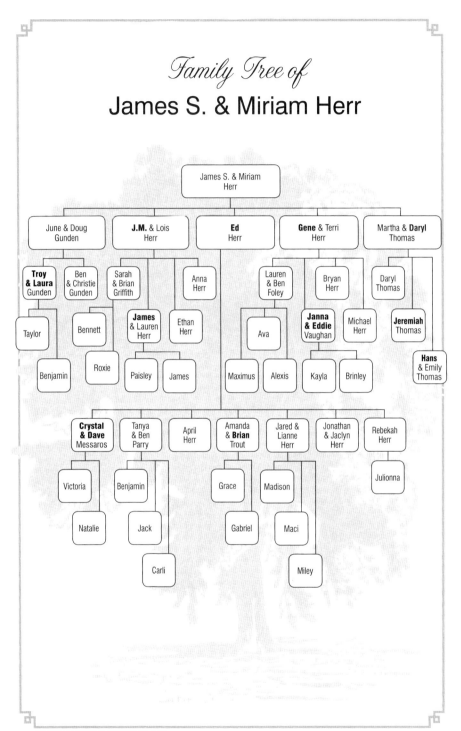

Milestones

1946	Bought Verna's Potato Chips for $1,750
1947	Moved business to a farm in Willow Street, PA
1949	Moved business to a bakery in West Willow, PA
1951	Fire destroyed the bakery
1952	Bought property in Nottingham, PA and constructed building
1956	Built addition for warehouse
1961	Incorporated
1962	Developed Panama business relationship
1963	Built new plant in Nottingham
1963	Employees Profit Sharing Trust was started
1966	First $1,000,000 sales year
1966	Opened 1st branch, Egg Harbor, NJ
1968	Built new plant in Nottingham
1973	Somerset, NJ branch was opened
1976	Began cheese curl production
1977	Purchased Carroll's Potato Chips in Chillicothe, OH
1977	Perryopolis, PA & Chillicothe, OH branches were opened
1978	Began popcorn production
1979	Jim Herr became President of the Snack Food Association
1980	Built new plant in Nottingham
1980	Wilkes-Barre, PA branch was opened
1981	Hampton, VA & Hatfield, PA branches were opened
1981	2nd generation family members join the Board of Directors

1981	Began pretzel production
1983	Name changed to Herr Foods Inc.
1983	Elkridge, MD branch was opened
1983	Began corn chip & tortilla chip production
1985	Herr Angus Farms was established
1986	Oakland, NJ branch was opened
1987	Camp Hill, PA, Lakewood, NJ & Seaford, DE branches were opened
1988	S. Philadelphia, PA branch was opened
1988	The James S. Herr Foundation was established
1989	Bedford, PA and Ona, WV branches were opened
1989	J.M. Herr was named President
1990	Corporate Office Center was built in Nottingham
1991	Jim Herr became Chairman of the National Federation of Independent Business (NFIB)
1992	Visitors Center was built in Nottingham
1992	New Castle, PA branch was opened
1993	Warehouse additions in Nottingham
1994	Jim Herr stars in TV Ads
1994	Newburgh, NY branch was opened
1996	Reach $100,000,000 in sales
1996	50th Year Anniversary celebrated
1997	Allentown, PA branch was opened
1997	Jim Herr receives the Circle of Honor Award from the Snack Food Association in recognition of outstanding contributions to the industry

1997	Jim Herr was named Business Leader of the Year by the PA Chamber of Business and Industry
1998	N. Philadelphia, PA branch was opened
1999	Addition to the Nottingham plant & 3rd chip line
2000	J.M. was named CEO; Ed Herr became company spokesman
2000	Concordville, PA branch was opened
2001	First non-family member joins Board of Directors
2004	Back to the future — began kettle chip production
2004	First national shipment to Wal-Mart
2005	Jim's title changed to Founder; J.M. Herr was named Chairman
2005	Ed Herr was named President
2006	60th Year Anniversary celebrated
2008	Plant II opened in Nottingham, with two production lines — one for extruded snacks & one for Baked Crisps
2009	Hainesport, NJ branch was opened
2010	The Nottingham Inn, an adjoining property & restaurant / lodging business, was acquired
2011	65th Year Anniversary celebrated
2013	Ten 3rd generation family members are working full time at the company
2013	Company purchased controlling interest in Silk City Snacks

SALES GROWTH

Year	Annual Net Sales Exceed ($)
1946	1,500
1956	150,000
1966	1,000,000
1976	10,000,000
1986	50,000,000
1993	100,000,000
2007	200,000,000
2013	250,000,000+

DISTRIBUTION ROUTES

Year	Number of Routes	Estimated Average Cost of Fuel/gallon ($)
1946	1	.15
1956	5	.22
1966	30	.32
1976	80	.59
1986	250	.89
1996	434	1.22
2006	505	2.96
2013	500+ Company owned routes; 250+ Distributor routes	3.45

PERSONNEL GROWTH

Year	Number of Employees*
1946	1½
1956	20
1966	75
1976	201
1986	630
1996	1,100
2006	1,366
2013	1,500+

*Full and Part Time

JAMES S. HERR, founder of Herr Foods Inc., has served as International President of the Snack Food Association, Chairman of the Board for the National Federation of Independent Business, Chairman of the Board of Interstate Drilling, Inc., Chairman of Sandy Cove Ministries, and President of the Oxford Area School District Board of Directors. He was named Outstanding Pennsylvania Businessman of the Year by the Small Business Association in 1969 and in 1997 he was named Businessman of the Year by the Pennsylvania Chamber of Business and Industry. He has received the highest honor bestowed on an individual by the Snack Food Association, in recognition of his contributions to the industry. In addition he has served on various community and ministry boards and has been active in his church all his life. On April 5, 2012, the 65th anniversary of his marriage to the former Miriam Hershey, James S. Herr died from complications of pneumonia. Together they had five children, twenty grandchildren, and twenty-two great-grandchildren.

BRUCE E. MOWDAY is an author of books on history, business, sports and true crime. He began his writing career as a newspaper reporter, columnist, and editor. He has won awards for investigative journalism, and hosted radio shows on three stations. He also regularly contributes to several magazines. Since 1997 he has been President of The Mowday Group, Inc., a full-service media relations firm headquartered in Chester County, Pennsylvania. For more information on Bruce Mowday, his books, and The Mowday Group, Inc., visit www.mowday.com.

JUNE HERR GUNDEN is a daughter of James S. Herr. Collaborating with her husband Doug, she helped her father create his autobiography. June and Doug are the owners of Peachtree Editorial Service, which specializes in serving Bible publishers worldwide. The company employs 25 people and is located in Peachtree City, Georgia.